To the Regions Beyond

by Rev. John Spillenaar

Published by
ACTS BOOKS
2165 Devlin Dr.
Burlington, ON.
L7P 3C6

Spillenaar, John, 1916-
To the regions beyond

Includes index.
ISBN 0-88941-028-3
1. Spillenaar, John, 1916- . 2. Native
peoples - Canada, Northern - Missions - History -
20th century, 3. Pentecostals - Canada, Northern -
Clergy - Biography. 5. Clergy - Canada, Northern -
Biography. I. Title.

BX8762.Z8S69 1992   266'.994'092   C92-094098-6

Contents

Foreword

Several years ago I remember reading in a church publication about a man who was flying into the Canadian north to bring the Gospel to its inhabitants. It was with admiration that I followed his activities whenever I could find information about him. I was sure it took real commitment to Jesus Christ to face the hazards and inconveniences of the north to preach the Good News. This was no ordinary man, but one truly called of God.

A few years later after the Lord led us into publishing, a letter arrived asking if we would be interested in doing a book for John Spillenaar, this person we had so admired. It was easy to know the Lords' direction in this request and soon we were involved in his first book, *Wings of The Gospel* and were enjoying Christian fellowship with John and his wife Tyyne, whose whole goal in life is to serve Jesus Christ.

There has been sacrifice, danger, challenge and commitment involved in the many years the Spillenaars have served in the north. But never has there been a complaint from either one.

John retired about ten years ago, but that was only a formality, not stopping him from his true calling, the north. His desire was to go as far north as he could and in his retirement years this has been accomplished, bringing the Gospel to the Inuit communities including the one closest to the North Pole.

John not only preaches the Word, he practices it. You can not get near him without being touched by his powerful witness for Christ. As he travels by plane, many co-passengers come to Christ. Others are led to the Lord in terminals, on the street, in restaurants, at fishing spots, in homes, etc.

In *To the Regions Beyond,* John continues his diary of activities in the north where his other book left off. My heart has been thrilled as I see the many souls that are won in the evangelistic efforts of this dedicated preacher. I'm challenged by the testimonies of those who found Jesus and were delivered from drugs, alcohol and many other degenerating sins.

It's all because someone is willing to live and share the true love of Jesus Christ, and as you read through the pages of this book, not only will your heart be enriched, but your whole spiritual self will be encouraged by the life and actions of John Spillenaar.

Jack Chamberlin.

Chapter 1

Reaching Out

**2 Cor. 10:16. "To preach the gospel
in the regions beyond**

This new book *To The Regions Beyond,* is a sequel to my former book *Wings of the Gospel",* which gives a little glimpse of my life story up to January 1976. In the last chapter of that book I had announced a "New Challenge". Instead of retirement, the Lord led me to go further north than ever before. You see, God saved me at the age of 12 and called me while still in my teens to "Go north and preach the gospel." I obeyed the call of God and started walking north, as I had no car, no bicycle, not even a horse and buggy. That was in 1936.

It was the last day of November, 1936 that I reached Kirkland Lake, Ontario, and pastored our first church. I also met my wife there: Tyyne Nykanen, who conducted gospel meetings to the Finnish people. We were married January 15, 1938. We started many churches in Northern Ontario, in towns that we could reach by car or train. God blessed and many souls were saved.

After building the church at Hearst, Ontario, which at that time was the end of the road, God spoke to my heart to learn to fly and keep going further north by plane.

I obeyed the Lord and took my aeronautical course at the Moody Bible Institute in Chicago, Illinois during the winter of 1950. The Lord provided our first plane through the Stone Church in Toronto in the fall of that year. In the following years the Lord provided 6 planes from a PA-18 to the Cessna 185. The Lord also provided means to build many churches in northern Ontario and northern Manitoba, right up to the shores of the Hudson Bay.

It was January 14, 1976 that I resigned from the Northland Mission work, which we started in 1950. But that was not the end of our missionary ministry. Our prayer was, "Lord, what would Thou have us do?" The Lord used Karl Kristensen, a school teacher in the Canadian Arctic at Ivugivik, Quebec, where the Hudson Bay and Hudson Strait meets, to help get us into the Eskimo ministry.

I had been involved in a limited way with missionary work among the Eskimos since 1952, but now the Lord was leading into a greater ministry. That's when we launched the *Harvest Field Inc.* ministry. It was April 16, 1976 that Len Thirst of

Komoka, Ont., and I flew north to meet Karl Kristensen. God blessed the meetings at Ivugivik and a number of Eskimos accepted Jesus as their personal Saviour.

I had promised to help the Northland Mission. So much time in June, July and August 1976, was spent in flying my successor, Dale Cummins, throughout Northern Ontario, to get acquainted with the people in the many communities, and to fly teachers into different settlements to conduct Bible School. Also, we worked for many days on the plane, to keep it in flying condition and for the annual inspection for the renewal of the "certificate of airworthiness".

POVUNGNITUK

On September 13, 1976 I flew north on a commercial flight to Povungnituk in northern Quebec on the east coast of Hudson Bay. That same night a large crowd of Eskimos gathered in the home where I was staying. God blessed in a wonderful way, as the Holy Spirit touched many hearts. A good number accepted Jesus as Saviour. Others were healed by the power of God. That meeting lasted until 2 A.M. the next day.

Another great service was held on the 14th. till nearly midnight. It was on September 15th. that the Anglican Minister asked me to preach in his church. He had attended our house meetings. A large crowd filled the church and I preached on the "born again" experience. After the message, I gave the altar call for those who wanted to receive Jesus as their personal Savior. a good three quarters of the congregation came forward. What a precious time we had in the presence of the Lord as the people prayed for forgiveness of sins and to invite Jesus to come into their hearts.

September 16th. - another meeting was requested to be held in the Anglican church. Again the Holy Spirit worked in many hearts as others came forward to receive Jesus as Savior. That meeting lasted till near midnight. But the people were still anxious to hear more, so a big crowd gathered in the home where I was staying for another meeting which lasted till 4.20 next morning.

The weather was turning cold. It was snowing and blowing, which was normal for this time of year at this latitude.

On June 15th I had applied to the Canadian government to register our *Harvest Field* as a non-profit organization in order for us to issue official income tax receipts. It was slow going, so September 20th I telephoned the National Revenue Board that I would fly to Ottawa the next day to pick up the necessary documents. So it was on September 21st. that this matter was taken care of. All papers were ready when I walked into the Revenue office. I had landed in the Ottawa River just south of the city; took a taxi to the government building and had our business taken care of in short order. I was able to fly back to South Porcupine in the afternoon.

Each fall I took a few days off to hunt moose. In fact we lived on moose meat for about 30 years. The Lord really helped me to locate the moose, sometimes in just an hour or two. Other times we hunted 2 or 3 days before we had our winter's meat.

We also had to pull the plane out of the water before the weather got too cold, and remove the pontoons and install the wheel-ski combination. This would usually take from 2 to 4 days to complete the job.

It was in November of 1976 that I began work on my book *Wings of the Gospel*. The first printing of 4000 sold out quickly. We then ordered the second printing of 4000. We sold out some time ago and we have just received the third printing, which tells part of my life story up to 1976.

Mark 16:15
Jesus said, "Go ye into all the world, and preach the gospel to every creature."

My next missionary trip to the Arctic was on December 3rd., 1976. I flew north in a commercial flight to Povungnituk, Quebec. A large crowd gathered for a meeting which ended at 3 A.M. next morning - the people wanted to hear more of the Word. More souls were saved and sick bodies healed. To God be all the honor and glory!

December 4th.-I flew north to Sugluk on the Hudson Strait. A large crowd was waiting when we landed and they requested a meeting immediately. They had heard of what God was doing at Povungnituk and they wanted to share the great out-pouring of the Holy Spirit. Our meeting started at 2 PM. God blessed and a number of these precious Eskimos accepted Jesus as their personal Savior. After the regular meeting, a time of discussion followed. Questions were asked and Bible answers were given. This meeting continued until 1 AM next morning.

December 5th. was a cold day: 30 degrees below zero, with a strong biting wind blowing. Another great meeting with a full house of Eskimos, which ended at 12:30 next morning. Again God blessed and a few received Jesus as Savior.

December 6th. - 41 degrees below zero; a terrific blizzard raging. With the wind chill factor the temperature was near the 80 below zero mark. Many who had accepted Jesus, now requested prayer to be delivered from bad habits. God moved mightily as one by one, these sincere Eskimos were delivered from the power and bondage of Satan. This meeting lasted till 1:30 next morning.

December 7th was another cold day, as the people gathered for a time of Bible Study. They were anxious to know what the will of God was for their lives. What a time of prayer and seeking the Lord followed the teaching of God's Word - till 1 AM next morning.

December 8th. Austin Airways DC-3 arrived in a terrific snow blizzard. I wanted to fly to Ivugivik but weather conditions were so bad, we could not land, and so we flew on to Povungnituk. I was so tired on arrival, but the people insisted on a time of Bible Study. The house was packed full of people as we studied the Word. This meeting closed just after midnight.

December 9th. We were supposed to fly to Ivugivik but the blizzard raged all day long. By 7 PM we were into another Bible Study with those who had accepted Jesus. I was so tired, we insisted on closing that meeting at 10:30 PM.

December 10th. I asked the Eskimos how cold it was and they said, "It's way below zero with the wind chill factor." I had my heavy winter clothing on, but the wind chill went right through my body. Another Bible Study was requested, on water baptism and the work of the Holy Spirit in our lives. Great interest was shown, as questions were asked till 3 next morning.

December 11th and we are still at Povungnituk. People gathered in the home I was staying in, so we had an afternoon Bible Study, with a little break for some supper, then we started again from 6 PM to 11 PM.

December 12th. Sunday and it dawned cold but clear. I attended the Anglican Church morning service. They asked me to preach in the evening service and also in the young peoples' meeting after the regular service. Nine young men came forward to dedicate their lives for service. Quite a few followed us to the home where I stayed, for a time of fellowship, with many questions asked, till about 1 AM.

December 13th. The weather was quite good for flying, yet very cold. We flew south, stopping at many settlements, but at long last I reached home in South Porcupine, so thankful for the grace God had shown on this missionary trip.

Chapter 2

Back to the Arctic

**2 Thess. 3:10. "If any would not work,
neither shall he eat."**

Much work was waiting for me at home: the many letters which had to be answered, receipts to be sent out, our financial books to be brought up to date and balanced each month. But I thank the Lord for the health and strength He has given me to carry on. Quite a number of missionary meetings were held in different churches in southern Ontario and also in the United States. Between time, I worked on my first book "Wings of the Gospel".

Acts 13:4A So we, "being sent forth by the Holy Ghost, departed" on another missionary trip to the Arctic

I left home at South Porcupine, Ontario and flew north to Povungnituk, Quebec on April 17th., 1977. The people were waiting for me and requested a Bible Study meeting immediately. A good crowd gathered, and God blessed His Word to the hearts of these sincere Eskimo Christians.

April 8th. - I made arrangements to use the High School auditorium for a special meeting with Evangelist Bill Prankard at a later date. Another good meeting of Bible Study tonight which lasted till 12:30 AM.

April 9th. - Had a short Bible Study here this AM. Packed up and flew to Cape Dorset - across the Hudson Strait on Baffin Island. From here, north is called the High Arctic. Had my first service here in Cape Dorset in a lovely home. Quite a few Eskimos gathered on short notice. One elderly Eskimo woman accepted Jesus as her personal Savior.

April 10th. - Sunday, I met Udjualuk Etidloie, who interpreted for me last night, and we attended the Anglican Church morning service. I was asked to preach in the evening service and one man accepted Jesus. The Eskimos requested another meeting in the home where I was staying. Another woman was saved.

April 11th. - Udjualuk and I visited a few homes where people were sick. Udjualuk prayed for them, and some immediately were healed and got up. In these homes, other members of the family accepted Jesus as Savior. Our meeting tonight was held in the Community Hall, with a good crowd in attendance.

Three men came forward for salvation. After I returned to the home I was staying in, quite a number of Eskimos gathered in for another service, which lasted till after midnight.

I was so tired, and went quickly to sleep. But at 2:45 AM I was awakened by someone knocking on my bedroom door. Upon opening the door, I found this elderly woman who had accepted Jesus, with the interpreter. She said, "Come and help us." I found out that she had visited many homes and told the people what God had done for her. At last she reached a small shack of a young couple who had been on drugs and were fighting and much of the furniture had been broken. She told them of our meetings and the many wonderful things that God was doing. Finally the young man said to her, "You go and bring the preacher here." So I got dressed and followed to see what damage was done! Both of the young people could speak and read English. I talked to them and read many scriptures, and by 5 AM both of them accepted Jesus. Praise the Lord!

April 12th. - Tonight's meeting was held in another home, and one young mother accepted Jesus.

April 13th. - The young couple asked that we hold our meeting tonight in their home. The place was crowded. This young couple who were saved last night, were filled with the joy of the Lord. Now they said, "We have found the answer which we were seeking for." They told us how the white man had brought alcohol into this village of about 700 people. Then later on brought drugs, stating that taking these drugs would bring happiness and joy, but the opposite was the result.

April 14th. - I visited this young couple, and the man mentioned how wonderful it is to be saved, but he said one thing was wrong. I said, "Nothing is wrong - everything is right." But he insisted that one thing was wrong, so at last I asked him what he meant. He informed me that he had been on welfare for a long time, but now that he was a Christian he wanted his own job to support him. He had been all over the village looking for work but nothing was available, so that's what was wrong. The Holy Spirit spoke to my heart to turn to the scripture in Matthew 7:7 *"Ask, and it shall be given you."* I said, "Here, read this."

After he read it, he said, "But that does not say a job."

I said, "No, it doesn't specify a job; but whatever we need, we must ask Jesus for it."

He said, "Do you mean that we can pray now for a job, and I will get one, when there are no jobs available?"

I told him, "Jesus spoke these words, and Jesus does not lie. He will do what He has promised."

My friend said, "O.K. let's pray." After a short prayer I had to leave.

But in the afternoon I visited in another home, and my friend walked in, all exuberant with joy. He exclaimed, "What a miracle!"

I said, "What are you talking about?"

He said, "When you left my home today, the telephone rang and a white man said, 'be here at work at 8 AM'." So praise the Lord for answered prayer!

Another meeting was held this evening, and another fine young Eskimo lady accepted Jesus as Savior.

April 15th. - Still here in Cape Dorset on Baffin Island. Questions were asked about the possibility of building a Full Gospel Church here, as there are now a good number of "born again" Christians. Believing God to supply all our needs, as He promised, I said, "Yes. We will plan to ship all the materials up here by boat from Montreal as soon as the ice is out next spring."

Our Bible Study tonight was on the "Baptism of the Holy Spirit." This meeting continued till 12:30 AM next morning.

April 16th. - Austin Airways plane arrived and I flew south to Povungnituk. Another good Bible Study in a home till 12:15 AM.

April 17th. - A group of fine Eskimo singers practiced for the Bill Prankard meetings. The Prankard party should arrive tomorrow. I was able to visit and counsel many people today. Returned 12:30 AM.

April 18th. - The Prankard party arrived by Austin Airways plane. A large crowd attended in the school gym. When the altar call was given, quite a number went forward to receive Jesus. Also the power of God was present to heal sick bodies.

April 19th. - Another great meeting in the school gym, with a larger crowd in attendance. Many more accepted Jesus as Savior and also as their Healer. Thank God for the moving of the Holy Spirit.

April 20th. - Brother Bill Prankard and party had to return to Ottawa, so I flew home to South Porcupine.

John 9:4
"I must work the works of Him that sent me, while it is day: the night cometh, when no man can work."

Prepared for Missionary Flight to the Arctic

On July 9th, 1977 my wife Tyyne and I loaded supplies in our motorhome, for our trip to Mattagami Quebec. I had planned to use Mattagami as a base to operate from on my flights north to reduce the flying time, compared to South Porcupine. Tyyne would live in the motorhome while I would be gone up north. We drove as far as Amos, Quebec. Tyyne drove our car while I drove the motorhome.

July 10th. - Arrived in Mattagami. Set the motorhome in place at the seaplane base. A service was arranged in the Indian Hall. A fair crowd gathered on short notice. Three came forward to accept Jesus.

July 11th. - I purchased two 45 gallon drums of aviation fuel and moved them over to the seaplane base. We had a busy day. The three who accepted Jesus last night came to our motorhome for prayer and Bible Study.

July 12th. - I got on the bus, returned to Amos, Val d'Or, Rouyn, Kirkland Lake and South Porcupine, arriving near midnight.

July 13th. - I refuelled the plane, but the weather did not permit me to fly out.

July 14th. - Weather cleared up and I flew to Mattagami. Refuelled the plane, got my 24 aeronautical maps ready to fly to the High Arctic. But I must say something right now. For the past couple of years, I had the impression that it was time I should give up flying, especially on these long flights. Although my pilot's medical was good, I noticed that I tired much more quickly than before. I did not mind the short flights, but these long flights took a lot out of me. But yet, I kept going, and here I was planning the longest flight ever.

July 15th. - Heavy rain, low ceiling and fog. Tyyne and I visited a few families today.

July 16th. - Up at 6 AM and I took off at 6:50 AM. The weather is clearing up nicely. I arrived at Great Whale River, landed and refuelled. I contacted the weather station for weather farther north. They said 0-0, which means zero visibility and zero ceiling. Some of the Eskimos helped me to tie the plane to one of the buoys in the Great Whale River, where it empties into the Hudson Bay. I stayed with one of the Eskimo families that night. A few people gathered in and we had a wonderful service. Prayed for a few people for salvation and healing.

July 17th. - Sunday. We attended the English service at the Anglican Church. This afternoon and evening we held our own service in George Kokajuk's house where I am staying. After service we drove down and checked the seaplane. Everything is O.K.

July 18th. - The weather looks good, so George and I drove down to the seaplane base - but no plane was in sight. During the night a strong wind came up, and with the river current plus the tide waters, the plane had capsized. Immediately I remembered the impression I had - that I should not be flying these long trips. So I said, "Thank you Lord. I get Your message now."

With our 185 Cessna QDH under water, quite a crowd of Eskimos gathered around. Three canoe loads of us went out to see if we could raise the plane, it was still tied to the buoy, but we could not raise it.

The Quebec Hydro had quite a few men working on a survey to harness the Great Whale River for Hydro power. So I made my way up to this Camp and at last found the head man of this hydro project. After telling him of my plane under water, he said, "If you need any help, just let us know." I said, "That's why I am here now - we need help to get the plane out. He gathered six of his men, and one of their larger boats with an outboard motor, and sent a large fork lift machine along the shore, opposite where the plane was. It was a big job, but at last they got a strong rope attached to the plane and brought the other end of the rope to where I and a few hydro men were waiting on shore with the fork lift machine. We tied the rope to the fork lift and in just a few minutes the plane arose about half way out of the water. We were able to draw it closer and bring it right side up in the water. The floats rested on the bottom, but little by little we hauled it up on shore, to the high tide mark.

I telephoned the insurance company with the bad news. They assured me that is why we carried insurance, and that they would see the plane was restored to the condition it was before.

Then I phoned Orillia Airways in Orillia, who did most of the major work that I had to get done. Harry Stirk, the owner of Orillia Airways told me to make a list of the damaged parts and to phone him again. Quite a number of parts were damaged, so I phoned Orillia again with this list and they promised to fly up with the necessary parts.

I drained all the oil and water out of the engine and turned the propeller over by hand many many times. I filled the engine with new oil, checked all connections and touched the starter button. Praise the Lord, the engine roared to life as if nothing had happened. To me, this was a miracle of God.

July 19th. - Most of the instruments in the plane were now useless. I worked all day on the plane. Pumped water out of the pontoons. Took all my survival things out - to dry them out and if possible rescue some to use again. Had a good Bible Study meeting in this home where I am staying.

July 20th. - I expected Orillia Airways plane to arrive, but it did not come. I found out later they got about half way, but had to land and spend the night. Again we had a good Bible Study meeting.

July 21st. - Heavy fog and a very cold wind blowing. Had

another good time of fellowship - singing, prayer and Bible Study.

July 22nd. - Harry Stirk and Bill, both pilots and both aeronautical engineers, arrived from Orillia with the parts to replace the damaged ones on my plane. It didn't take long to replace these parts. At last Harry said, "O.K., the plane is ready for a test flight." I said, "Which one of you is going to make the test flight?" I had drained the gas tanks before and had refuelled the plane.

Harry said, "No, it's your plane, so you test fly it." I knew if Harry said it's O.K. to fly - I had confidence in his judgment. So I taxied out. Even though the ceiling was low, I could at least make a short flight. I took off and flew inland about 15 miles. There it was CAVU, which means Ceiling and Visibility Unlimited. Very good flying weather. So I flew back to the seaplane base and told Harry and Bill, "The weather is clear inland and we can fly out before dark."

He said, "O.K. John, you go on. We will go back to our plane at the airport, and since we are on wheels, we will fly faster than you and catch up with you in less than half an hour.

I took off and flew south. After a half an hour, I waited to hear from them on my radio which was still in working condition, but no call came. So I called them. They answered and asked where I was. I told them I was crossing a certain river. "Okay," they said, "We will soon catch up with you." A few clouds had gathered, as I waited for another half hour. I called them again and they asked, "Where are you now?" I gave them the name of another river I was then crossing. "Oh," they said, "We are not gaining on you at all. What altitude are you at?" I answered that my altimeter was not working , so I did not know how high I was flying. Harry asked, "What temperature does your guage read?" So I gave them the outside temperature. "Oh," they said, "That explains it. You are flying much higher than we are and you have a stronger tail wind." They never did catch up to me, as I landed back at Mattagami. They flew on south to Orillia that night as both of them are instrument pilots.

July 23rd. - Tyyne and I refuelled the plane and I flew to South Porcupine, removed everything out of the plane and refuelled.

July 24th. - I remember, while at Great Whale River getting the plane out of the water, one of the top Quebec Hydro men and I were talking together. At last he asked, "John, how can you be so peaceful, when your plane is under the water?"

I was able to tell him, "I have the Prince of Peace within me - Jesus." So I had a wonderful opportunity to witness to him about the love of God.

I got my ticket and rode the bus back to Mattagami. Had a good talk with a Catholic priest who sat beside me. He appeared interested and asked many questions. So the Lord only knows the results of the seed sown.

July 25th. - Tyyne drove our car and I the motorhome on the all day trip back to South Porcupine.

July 26th. - I got up at 5 AM. Daniel my son drove me to the airport. I took off at 6:15 and flew the damaged plane to Orillia for a complete overhaul. Harry Stirk and one of his flight instructors and I flew back to Timmins in a small twin Cessna.

Mark 16:16 "He that believeth and is baptized shall be saved; but he that believeth not shall be damned."

August 11th, 1977 - I got up at 3:45. Tyyne took me to Timmins Airport. We took off in Austin Airways 748 Hawker Siddley. We flew to Kapuskasing, Great Whale, Frobisher Bay, Pangnirtung, back to Frobisher Bay and on to Cape Dorset. A good crowd gathered for service, which lasted till 12:45 AM. God blessed and some came forward for salvation.

August 12th. - Prepared for a water baptismal service in the icy waters of a small lake behind the village. This is the first water baptism by immersion here. Many were warned against it, but five Eskimo adults were baptized. The evening service was held in the school education center. A good crowd attended, wanting to hear the testimonies of those who followed the Lord in water baptism. It was a wonderful service.

August 13th. - I flew to Sugluk in Austin's Twin Otter. Quite a few people gathered and we had a great time of praise and worship before our Bible Study.

August 14th. - Sunday. We attended the morning service at the Anglican Church. Many Eskimos requested an afternoon service in a home. We had a great time of worship together. Then another service in the evening in another home. These folk love the freedom of worship in our meetings - instead of a formal ritual.

August 15th. - Visited a few homes; bought groceries at the Hudson Bay store. A large crowd gathered for the evening service at 7:30 till after 1 AM. Many took part in discussion of water baptism and the coming of the Lord. A great time of prayer followed.

August 16th. - Still in Sugluk. Austin Airways Canso plane came in and landed on the water. We flew to Povungnituk. Had a great time in the evening service in the Presence of the Lord. Many came up for prayer.

August 17th. Yesterday we had wanted to fly to Ivugivik but

the weather did not allow a landing there. Today we flew to Ivugivik. One of our Christian men, who accepted the Lord in our first meetings here, asked if I wanted to go for a trip in his speed boat to an island about 14 miles away in the Hudson Bay. I accepted his offer. We reached the island in a short time. Lucassie, my Eskimo friend, checked some things, while I took a walk on the beach.

In a few minutes he called, "Let's go." I ran back and got in the speedboat, while he pushed off with a paddle.

Lucassie tried to start the outboard. It refused to start. This was about 9:30 in the morning, and I had had a black cup of coffee before leaving Povungnituk. Lucassie worked hard on that motor all day till 5 PM. He told me, there is lots to eat here: this plant is good, and that one too, and this sea weed is good - but really I wasn't too hungry. At last Lucassie said, "O.K., we must climb to the top of the cliff." He shouldered a 10 gallon keg of gas and started to climb. I followed. At long last we reached the top. He found a concave place in the surface stone. "Let's gather moss," he said. So we gathered a huge pile of moss - he placed a lot of moss in this concave spot. "Now," he said, "We must wait till it's dark." At about 10:30 PM Lucassie poured half of the gas on the moss, then threw a lighted match onto it, and a great fire roared. Lucassie said, "This is a signal to the people back in Ivugivik." After about 25 minutes, the fire had died down. We piled the rest of the moss in the concave place. He threw the rest of the gas on it, and threw a lighted match on it. Again it burst into a huge flame. "O.K.," Lucassie said, "Let's walk back down." We had brought a flashlight and I stumbled behind Lucassie as we made our way down the very steep hill. About half way down, Lucassie said, "Listen, I can hear them coming." I couldn't hear them but he did. By the time we reached the water, the speedboat arrived. Was I ever glad to be back in the village, just a little after midnight. Lucassie fried polar bear steak for our meal.

August 18th. - I visited a few homes. Had Arctic char to eat. A very good service in Lucassie's home and a good crowd attended. Prayer for deliverance of bad habits, also a few requested and prayed for salvation.

August 19th. - 24th. Still at Ivugivik. Had a wonderful time sharing the Good News in many homes. Then meetings each night - Bible teaching with the new believers.

August 25th. - Austin's Canso plane arrived and landed in the water in front of the village. We flew to Povungnituk quite late in the afternoon. A cold evening breeze was blowing. Five Inuit men and women asked me to baptize them in water by immersion, as the Bible teaches. We walked back behind the village to a little lake, and in spite of the icy waters and cold breeze, we had a marvellous Baptism service. Then another Bible Study and teaching till 11:30 PM.

August 26th. - Flew home to South Porcupine.

Chapter 3

Another Direction

Missionary Trip Through Mexico and Central America

I had purchased a motorhome on June 3rd., 1977 in London, Ontario. Now on October 31st., 1977 we left South Porcupine to begin our trip south. Our son Daniel, Tyyne and I drove to Kirkland Lake and visited our daughter Grace and her husband Glen Adams and family. Our next stop was North Bay, then on through to Toronto where we visited friends.

November 2nd. - We crossed the U.S. Border at Lewiston, N.Y. and had a nice overnight visit with my older brother Matthew and his wife Rita.

November 3rd. - We drove to Akron, Ohio and attended Grace Cathedral, Ernest Angley, pastor, also the large church of Rex Humbard and the Assembly of God where Rev. Meandor pastored.

November 7th. - We left Akron, Ohio and drove through to Mansfield, Ohio to visit our friends Frank and Helen Hock, the pastor and his wife, Don Holtzapple of the large Diamond Hills Baptist Church. While here, Frank Hock purchased a C.B. radio and installed it in our motorhome for our trip through Mexico and Central America.

November 12th. - About 70 men and women gathered for a breakfast meeting at the Diamond Hills Baptist Church. I shared with them some of my experiences in the north, plus a message from the Word of God. Many of these men, and pastor Don Holtzapple himself, came up north and helped us build a number of churches. They would drive as far as possible, then I would fly them in the rest of the way. After this breakfast meeting, we continued our journey south.

We stopped at PTL in North Carolina where I was on the TV program.

November 15th. - We visited our friends, Joe and Marilyn Luce, at the Blue Bird Bus and motorhome plant in Fort Valley, Georgia.

November 17th. We arrived at Lake Worth, Florida, and immediately went for a swim in the Atlantic Ocean. It was 80 degrees F. temperature. Visited many homes for the next few days and shared the gospel message.

November 20th. I was requested to preach the Sunday morning service at the Finnish Pentecostal Church. My wife Tyyne interpreted for me and also shared a good testimony.

November 23rd. - In Fort Lauderdale, Pastor George Miller of the Oakland Park Assembly Church, had me preach and also I shared about the work in the North.

December 3rd. - Found us at the Christian Retreat in Bradenton, Fl. It was a Saturday night and their speaker failed to show up, so they asked me to preach and share what God was doing in the Canadian Arctic. After the service, we sold about 60 of my book *"Wings of the Gospel"*.

December 8th. - We left Florida and drove through Alabama, Mississippi, into Louisiana. We always stopped for a service on Sunday morning, drove through Sunday afternoon, and stopped for a service in some church for the Sunday evening. We also planned on attending some church for the weekly Wednesday night meeting.

December 10th. - We arrived at Brownsville, Texas, where we had arranged with our post office in South Porcupine to forward our mail. It took us a few days to answer the mail. We also took out insurance to travel through Mexico. We emptied our holding tank, filled our water tank, checked tires and batteries, filled propane tank and did our laundry; then changed U.S. money into Mexican money.

December 16th. - Started our trip through Mexico. We were able to get hundreds of gospel tracts in Spanish to distribute.

December 18th. - We crossed over from the eastern coast of Mexico to Juchitan on the Pacific coast. Met some folks from Mesa, Arizona and had a nice service together. We were able to distribute many gospel tracts in Spanish, and the people appeared very pleased to receive them.

December 21st. - We reached the border of Guatemala where we purchased more insurance to pass through this Central American country.

December 23rd. - Here we are in San Salvador. We parked on the Bible School grounds and met some of the U.S. missionaries.

December 25th. - Christmas evening. I was asked to preach in a large church here where John Bueno is pastor. He interpreted for me.

December 26th. - We left San Salvador and drove through Honduras, giving out Spanish tracts as we went. We arrived in Nicaragua by nightfall. All these Central American countries have their own currency, so it kept us busy trying to figure out the money, when we stopped to purchase fuel and groceries. But the Lord helped us and I noticed people were very co-operative after I gave them gospel tracts. Men and women were so courteous as they pressed through the crowds that would gather, to ask for more tracts.

December 28th. - Crossed over a mountain 11,050 feet high

and descended to enter Panama. In all these countries we not only had to take out insurance and exchange money, but we also had to get visas for each of us. But the Lord really helped and we had no trouble at all. We were quick however to give out these Spanish tracts first, before doing any business.

December 29th. - Now in Panama City, after crossing the Panama Canal. We watched as huge ships passed through the locks, from the Atlantic Ocean to the Pacific and vice versa.

January 1st., 1978. - Panama City, Panama. We met some fine people here. Some could speak English and we were able to witness to quite a few people, who appeared to be anxious to know more about the gospel.

January 3rd. - We crossed the border into Costa Rica at 4:30 PM on our return trip.

January 4th. - While shopping, the building began to shake and quiver and all the people rushed outside, so we followed them. It was a big earthquake. It did a lot of damage to buildings, but I did not hear of anyone killed.

January 5th. - We left Costa Rica and entered Nicaragua. Here we met some lovely people who could speak English and we had a great time witnessing to them about the Lord Jesus Christ. We passed through one area which was struck by a severe earthquake in 1972. More than 20,000 people were reported killed and huge buildings were levelled.

January 6th. - We crossed over the small country of Honduras and into El Salvador. We only wanted to drive during the daylight hours. Many animals and even people would lay down to sleep on the highways.

January 7th. - We arrived back at the Bible Institute in San Salvador, where we took part in the evening service.

January 8th. - Helen Egler, who had accompanied us from here to Panama and back, now had to get back to her teaching job. As this is Sunday, we attended the large Evangelistic Center services.

January 10th. - Crossed the border into Guatemala. We found all these people throughout Central America very friendly and receptive to the gospel message.

January 11th. - Drove to Guatemala City, which is a climb from sea level to 4800'. We visited the Blue Bird Bus plant and met many U.S. missionaries at a conference. We accepted another large box of gospel tracts in Spanish.

January 13th. - We crossed the border into Mexico. All through Central America, there were many roadblocks, manned by the military with sub-machine guns. We would stop our motorhome and I'd get a handful of Spanish tracts and go out and hand these soldiers tracts. After looking at the tracts, some soldiers would hold up five fingers, indicating he wanted five more tracts, others three, and so on. Then we would drive on through the road blocks. We had no trouble at all; although we were warned in the States not to attempt this trip at all, and if we did go we would have plenty of trouble.

January 14th. - We travelled up the west side of Mexico along the Pacific Ocean. It was very mountainous but beautiful. Again we distributed hundreds of gospel tracts, which had an address on each one, where to write for further information.

January 15th. - Arrived in Mexico City. I believe it is over 9000' altitude, and we were told it's the largest city in the world. We visited market places teeming with people, gratefully accepting our gospel tracts. We parked for the nights, just any place, perhaps on a side street or beside a gas station, and we never had any problems.

January 19th. - We crossed the Arizona border at Nogales, where we found a large bundle of mail waiting for us at the main post office. Answered mail for the next few days.

January 22nd. - Sunday. We found an Assembly of God church here with a large parking lot, so I've been answering our mail the last few days, and now we can attend the services here. Many of the letters requested my book *"Wings of the Gospel"*, which I was able to mail out from here.

January 25th. - After checking the motorhome for fuel, propane. water, etc., we drove on toward California.

January 26th. - We crossed into California State at 10:30 AM. and drove on through San Diego to visit a Finnish woman, who came over from Finland on the same ship that Tyyne came on. The last time they met was 48 years ago. We attended good gospel services in a few churches here, also the Full Gospel Business Men's Banquet.

January 30th. - We left San Diego area and drove north.

February 1st., 1978 - In the Los Angeles area - visited Rev. John Scarr. We had him come to pastor the church at Wawa, Ontario years ago. He now has a lovely church here in Downey, a suburb of Los Angeles. I preached in his church tonight. Many came forward for prayer, when the altar call was given.

February 2nd. - We visited Dr. Schuller's church at Garden Grove. I was on the Melodyland TV program.

February 3rd. - Visited Jack McAllister's World Literature Crusade headquarters. Also visited the Skelton family home in Granada Hills. Dr. Skelton has a good practice here. Mrs. Skelton, who was Lillian Kivi, was a little girl in the Val d"Or, Quebec area, and later at New Liskeard, where she received her training as a nurse.

February 5th. - Lillian Skelton took us to Jack Hayford's church in Van Nuys, where big crowds attended the four services each Sunday.

February 7th. - Drove north to Santa Barbara. Visited Hilda Hendrickson, another Finnish lady who came from Finland about the same time as my wife, Tyyne.

February 8th. - Wednesday. We attended Rev. Cowie's church. I shared in the service and showed my slides of the Eskimos.

February 9th. - Drove north to San Francisco. Visited another Finnish lady, a friend of Tyyne's 48 years ago, Hilja Salonen.

February 10th. - Drove over the Golden Gate bridge and visited the Redwood forest, some trees over 2000 years old. Drove east to Modesto to another Canadian family, Albert and Anita Vaters. Anita was a little girl in our South Porcupine church when we pastored there; later she became our pianist. There are hundreds of acres of beautiful almond nut trees in full blossom.

February 12th. - Sunday. Albert Vaters asked me to speak to the Sunday School and also preach in the evening service. A large group responded to the altar call and came forward for prayer.

February 14th. - Picked up our mail here and answered many letters. I showed my slides of the Canadian Arctic in the evening service.

February 15th. - 17th. -Drove south to the Los Angeles area. I had wanted to drive east from Modesto to Oklahoma, but was advised not to, because of heavy snow in the mountains.

February 18th. - Saturday. I shared in the Full Gospel Business Men's breakfast here in Granada. We parked our motorhome in Dr. and Mrs. Skelton's yard.

February 19th. - Lillian Skelton took us to the large Los Angeles Temple built by Amie McPherson. Howard Courtney is now pastor. Tyyne took quite a case of angina here. Dr. Skelton examined her and she spent the night in the hospital.

February 20th. - 25th. - Drove on toward Palm Springs. We were able to witness to many people along the way, and distributed gospel literature.

February 26th. - Sunday. Attended the Assembly of God church. Met Canadian Frank Reed of Toronto Stone Church. I was asked to bring a brief message.

February 27th. - We left California and drove east into Arizona to Sun City, a beautiful retirement area where hundreds of senior citizens come to live.

March 1st., 1978 - Found us at Flagstaff, Arizona where we visited the Grand Canyon. Flagstaff is approximately 7000' altitude.

March 2nd. - 4th. - Drove through the desert to El Paso, Texas, a city of about 500,000 population. We met some very nice people here and were able to share the gospel with many.

March 5th. - 8th. - Arrived at Dallas, Texas. Refuelled motorhome with gas at .49 cents a gallon. Visited a Rev. Frank Slater, a friend of my father's of many years ago. Snow flurries.

March 9th. - Drove north to Tulsa, Oklahoma. A large bundle of mail was here for us. We visited Tommy Osborn's head office and the Oral Roberts complex.

March 10th. - 12th. - Answered the mail. Attended Faith Chapel. The pastor asked me to preach in the PM service. A large crowd attended and many came forward for prayer.

March 13th. - 14th. - Left Oklahoma and arrived in Missouri. Colder weather as we travelled north. 36 degrees F.

March 15th. - Arrived in Chicago, Ill. Visited some of our friends. Good opportunity to witness for the Lord.

March 16th. - Visited Earl Bergman in Benton Harbor, Michigan. I had taken Earl with me on a two week flight into the Arctic twelve years ago.

March 21st. - Crossed the border into Ontario at Windsor. Visited a few of our friends. The Finish church pastor asked me to preach in his church.

March 24th. - Drove to Kitchener to our youngest son David's home. Attended the Good Friday service at the Waterloo Pentecostal church. Visited many friends in this area.

March 27th - April 11th., 1978 - Visited my sister Cora in Toronto, my oldest brother in St. Catharines, and second oldest brother Matthew, in Lewiston, N.Y. Back to Toronto to speak in Brother Derkatch's church. Then up to Gooderham to my younger sister's home, Alida Dewey, also my sister Ruth in Lindsay. We stopped in New Liskeard and visited the Kivi's, parents of Lillian Skelton of California, Glen and Grace Adams in Kirkland Lake and arrived in South Porcupine, Ontario, where 2 1/2 feet of snow filled our driveway. I hired a front end loader to take the snow away.

Chapter 4

A New Project

**Mark 16:20 "The Lord working with them, and confirm-
ing the word with signs following."**

April 27th., 1978. South Porcupine, Ontario. We got up at
3:25 AM, breakfasted and finished packing for a missionary
trip to the Canadian Arctic. Dan drove me to the Timmins airport. Took off with a full load of groceries at 5 AM in Austin
Airways 748, a 50 passenger plane. We landed twice enroute
to Cape Dorset and arrived there at 12 noon.

Many Christians gathered in Udjualuk's home for a Bible
teaching on Christian living.

April 28th. - I stayed in the home of Jerry Siemens, a
Christian contractor, who was here on Baffin Island building
houses for the native people, under the Northwest Territories
government contract. He had three white men with him who
also were carpenters. Our evening service was held in an
Eskimo schoolteacher's home. Again, it was a profitable time
of Bible teaching on the life Jesus wants us to live.

April 29th. - A very cold wind blowing, which brought the
temperature down to about 40 below zero with the wind chill
factor. Today, we held a meeting about building a church here
at Cape Dorset. A few of us went to the town office and
talked to the mayor and some of the town council. Permission
was granted for us to build a Full Gospel church here.

In the afternoon I flew to Sugluk in Austin's Twin Otter
plane. Sugluk is on the south shore of Hudson Strait in the
province of Quebec. A good crowd of Eskimos gathered for
our Bible teaching - the meeting ended at midnight.

April 30th. - Sunday - We attended the Anglican Church service this morning. Visited in a few homes, had Bible reading
and prayers. Another Bible Study this evening. Snowing and
blowing all day.

May 1st., 1978 - Here in Sugluk, Quebec. I am staying in one
of the Eskimo Christian's homes. These native people do not
mind being called Eskimo: this name means "raw meat eater";
but they prefer to be called Inuit which means "the people of
the land". Our Bible Study tonight ended after midnight, as
the Christians are anxious to learn more of what the Bible
teaches.

May 2nd. - Tuesday, the people asked for another Bible
Study this morning before I leave. We had a precious time to-

gether, as questions were asked and answers given from the Bible verses. Austin's Twin Otter arrived and I flew to Povungnituk. Another good Bible Study here, till after midnight.

May 3rd. - The Anglican Church minister asked to have our Bible Study in his home here in POV. This meeting lasted till midnight.

May 4th. - Austin's Twin Otter took off at 8 AM. One of the Inuit men took me to the plane. We landed at Port Harrison, the Belcher Islands, Great Whale River, Paint Hills, Eastmain, Moosonee, Timmins, and I was home again.

Nehemiah 2:20 "The God of heaven, He will prosper us; therefore we His servants will arise and build."

May 10th. - Prepared motorhome for trip to Montreal to purchase building supplies for the church at Cape Dorset on Baffin Island, N.W.T., and arrange for the shipping. Arrived in North Bay by nightfall.

May 11th. - Up at 6:15 AM., drove through to Ottawa. Contacted Bro. Bill Prankard about building the church at Cape Dorset.

May 12th. - Friday - Arrived in Montreal early and I telephoned many different lumber companies comparing prices on materials; also to furniture stores for parsonage furniture.

May 13th. - Drove to Pascal furniture store and ordered a fridge., kitchen table and chairs, beds, dressers and living room furniture.

May 14th. - Sunday - We attended Evangel Temple for Sunday School and morning service. Rev. Weller is pastor. Mr. and Mrs. Viljo Korhonen took us to the church in Verdun for the evening service. Rev. Robert and Wally Johnson are pastors.

May 15th. - Drove to the lumber company and ordered all the building supplies for the church in Cape Dorset on Baffin Island, N.W.T. Ordered chairs for the church and also an oil heater.

May 16th. - Received $16,000.00 from Rev. Bill Prankard to help pay for all those supplies. I drove to the Montreal Harbor and made arrangements to ship these supplies to Cape Dorset. We attended a Finnish church meeting in a home. I was requested to speak.

May 17th. - We left Montreal and drove to Ottawa, Renfrew, Bancroft and to Gooderham. Parked our motorhome at Frank and Alida Dewey's. Alida is my younger sister. They have millions of bees and keep us supplied in honey all year.

May 18th. - Up at 5:30 AM. Drove to North Bay, then to

Kirkland Lake. Visited Glen and Grace and family. We took Joy and Timmy with us. Arrived home in South Porcupine at 5 PM.

May 24th. - June 2nd. Worked on plane, C of A inspection, changed oil, cleaned inside and outside, waxed, etc.

June 3rd., 1978 - June 30th. - We were in Southern Ontario where I preached in different churches.

July 1st., 1978 - I flew to Attawapiskat where we had built the last church. Dan Tomen of London, Ontario had purchased a good size generator, 4000 watts, to produce electricity, so we could use power tools in building churches. We loaded the heavy generator into the plane, to be taken to Cape Dorset, N.W.T.

July 6th. - I flew to Cape Dorset in Austin Airways plane, as the Montreal shipping company had informed us that their ship would arrive at Cape Dorset with all the materials for the church building. When we arrived, we noticed solid ice three miles out, where the ship was anchored. Had a good Bible teaching in one of the Inuit's homes.

July 7th. -Udjualuk and I met with the housing committee and arranged to have the church site prepared to build on. Another very good service tonight.

July 8th. - Elijah Pootoolik and his family agreed to move out of their home, so when our men came up to build, we could all stay together. Austin's plane flew me across Hudson Strait, on south to the Great Whale River. I stayed in Apilie Napartuk's home. July 9th. - Had good opportunities to witness and share the good news of salvation.

July 10th. Austin's plane arrived and we flew south, stopping at many villages along the way. Landed at Timmins at 5:30 PM. Tyyne picked me up.

July 10th. - 15th. - Bought a lot of groceries to take to Cape Dorset to feed the men building the church.

July 25th. - I've been waiting for a phone call from Cape Dorset about ice conditions. Word came today that the ice is breaking up and moving out.

July 26th. - I purchased plane tickets for six men who were coming to help us build at Cape Dorset. I took Arne Lindholm and Carl Haacke from South Porcupine to Timmins Airport at 10:30 PM.

July 27th. - At last the plane took off at 1:30 AM and we arrived at Cape Dorset at 9 AM. We all moved into Elijah's house. We went to work preparing the site to build on. We worked till 12:30 AM next morning.

July 28th. - We were up at 7 AM. I was chief cook and dish washer. On the job at 8 AM. Temperature four degrees C. The ground was frozen solid We picked and shovelled all day using wheel barrows to move the earth away. We made up three sills

48' long, by spiking 2 X 8's together.

July 29th. - Built frames 3" X 3" for concrete pads. Jerry, the Christian contractor, brought a cement mixer over, and we filled ten pads with concrete.

July 30th. - Sunday. Rev. Bill Prankard and party arrived. A good big crowd gathered in the Community Center on short notice. Many Inuits came forward for prayer: some for salvation, others for healing.

July 31st. - Up at 6 AM. Poured the concrete into the remaining pads. Bill Prankard's crew took a video of us working. They left to fly south at 11:30 AM. Peter Laukkanen piloted a rented plane.

August 1st and 2nd., 1978 - Floor joists were nailed to the sills; cleat nailed to the floor joists to hold in floor insulation. Four Inuit men worked along with us. We quit work at 8:30 PM.

August 3rd. - John Wheeler from Matheson, David Maves and son and Jeff Foss and son arrived from Pembroke to help us build. Worked all day on the church.

August 4th. - Up at 6:45. Finished insulating the floor - put 3/4" plywood flooring on. Made up the four walls on the floor, and raised them into place.

August 5th. - Built roof trusses and installed into place. Sheeted in the north side with plywood. Started to shingle.

August 6th. - Sunday. I phoned Jim White in Sarnia. He plans to come up and install all electrical material. I preached in the AM and PM services. A large crowd attended and a few came forward to accept Jesus as Savior, others for prayer.

August 7th. - Completed the room by noon. Built partition in pastor's apartment: two bedrooms, washroom, kitchen and living room. Started to install plywood ceiling and insulation.

August 8th. - Up at 6:30 AM. Worked on ceiling and insulation; sheeting on outside walls. Started to stain exterior walls.

August 9th. - Put finishing touches on exterior of building. Held dedication service for the new church building.

August 10th. - Jim and Lena White arrived from Sarnia at 9 AM. Worked on electrical work till 8:30 PM. Arne Lindholm built front steps. Udjualuk painting the ceiling. Many neighbours stated they never saw a building go up so fast.

August 11th. - Six of our men packed up to fly south. Jim White worked in electrical wiring.

August 12th. - Men waited at airport till early this morning when Austin's plane arrived. Arne Lindholme and I did odd jobs around and helped Jim with wiring.

August 13th. - Sunday. I preached at the AM service; about 50 attended. In the PM I showed Lester Sumrall's film and over 100 attended.

August 14th. - Arne and I built bedroom closets. Jim completed all electrical work.

August 15th. - We were asked to be at the airport at 4 AM. We packed and had all our things at the airport. Austin's plane arrived at 8:30 AM - but had to fly north to Pond Inlet.

August 16th. - Zero degrees temperature. Waited all day for plane return flight. Held PM service in a home.

August 17th. - Austin's 748 plane arrived. We all flew south. Mission accomplished.

September 4th., 1978 - In Montreal, Dorval airport. Took off in Nordair plane; flew north to Fort Chimo. Visited two homes.

September 5th. - Air Inuit plane took off at 10:15 AM. We flew to Payne Bay, Koartak and Wakeham Bay - snowing. Good evening service, about 60 people attended. When I gave the altar call, many came for prayer.

September 6th. - Wakeham. Our Christians here requested a church to be built next summer. Pastor Joseph and I met with the Mayor and Town Council. Good PM service in Joseph's home - Bible teaching.

September 7th. - We surveyed site for a church building. I talked to the school principal. He requested I send English and French New Testaments to school students. Another good meeting of Bible teaching.

September 8th. - Out about 6 AM. Went with two Inuit men for a quick seal hunt - shot one. They ate most of it for breakfast right there, but I wasn't hungry. Met with Council - Mayor opposed to another church. PM service in Pappi's home, till 12:20 AM.

September 9th. - Another Bible Study all morning. Agreed to build church next summer. I flew to Fort Chimo.

September 10th. Sunday. One white couple and I attended the Anglican service. This couple requested water baptism. Baptismal service in the Fort Chimo river - very cold.

September 11th. - Flew back to Montreal. Tyyne and I drove motorhome to Ottawa.

September 12th. - Up at 3 AM; started to drive north. Visited at North Bay and Kirkland Lake. Arrived home in South Porcupine at 7:30 PM.

Luke 14:28 "For which of you, intending to build a tower, sitteth not down first, and counteth the cost, whether we have sufficient to finish it?"

November 2nd., 1978 - Made a trip to London, Ont. Contacted Hilltop Motors re: building two units for a church building in Wakeham Bay. Each unit 12' wide by 44' long. We agreed on a price and they promised to have them ready in the spring.

Missionary Itinerary in Southern Churches

November 5th. - Sunday. I shared about the Arctic work in the Assembly of God church in Lewiston, N.Y. in both morning and evening services.

November 8th. - I spoke in the mid week meeting in the Assembly of God church here in State College, Pa.

November 12th. - I shared in the PM service at the Diamond Hills Baptist church in Mansfield, Ohio.

November 24th. - We are now at the Christian Retreat in Bradenton, Florida. I was asked to speak at the 8:30 AM service - fair crowd.

November 25th. - Requested to share news of the Canadian Arctic missionary work in the 9:30 and 10:30 AM services here at Christian Retreat.

December 3rd., 1978 - Sunday. Lakeland, Florida - Gunnar Kars, a Canadian, is pastor of Trinity Assembly of God church. He asked me to preach in the PM service.

December 6th. - Deland, Florida. I preached in the mid-week service in the Assembly of God Church.

December 10th. - In Lake Worth, Florida. I preached in the Finnish Pentecostal church in the evening service.

December 27th. - Wednesday. Rev. Hollingsworth, pastor of the Assembly of God in Seminole, Florida asked me to preach.

December 28th. - At Crystal River, Florida at the Norvel Hayes Conference. I shared in the 10 AM service about the Arctic missionary work.

December 30th. - I shared in the missionary meeting at the Christian Retreat, Bradenton, Florida this afternoon.

January 4th., 1979. - Lake Worth, Florida. I preached in the evening service in the Finnish Pentecostal Church. Big crowd. A few came forward for salvation.

January 6th. - I contacted Hilltop Motors in London, Ont. by phone about the two units they were to build for our church in Wakeham Bay. They informed me they were too busy to build them.

Tyyne took me to Miami airport and I flew up to Timmins, Ontario. I contacted our accountant, Ron Campbell about the 1978 audit of our Harvest Field financial books. Temperature was minus 28 degrees C.

January 10th. - I flew from Timmins to Toronto to Montreal. Mr. Walter Miller met me at the airport and I stayed in their home.

January 11th. - Walter and I went to Atco Company about

building two units for the church at Wakeham Bay. We put all details on paper and agreed on size and price. I was told they would build them according to agreed specifications and have them ready for spring. I paid a deposit on this order. He promised to have all this typed out and sent to me in Florida for my signature.

January 12th. - I flew to Toronto. Met with Brother Bill Prankard and we discussed the Wakeham Bay church.

January 14th. - I flew to Miami. Tyyne met me at the airport.

February 3rd., 1979 - Ivan Spillenaar, my oldest brother's son, phoned that Jim his father died last night. We had prayed for Jim's salvation every day for many years. When I visited Jim, I could talk about flying, about Eskimos, but as soon as I started to talk about the Lord, Jim would say, "If that's what you came to see me about, there's the door, you can go." Many times I was so discouraged - and now Jim had died. I made reservations to fly to Buffalo and take a bus to St. Catharines.

February 4th. - Sunday - Lake Worth, Florida. I was asked to preach in the Finnish Pentecostal church - a large crowd. Many came forward for prayer.

February 5th. - I flew on Eastern Airways from West Palm Beach airport to Buffalo, N.Y. Took a bus to St. Catharines. I stayed at Ed and Vaneta Wills, Jim's daughter.

February 6th. - Attended Jim's funeral service. The minister said a gentleman had a few words to say. It was Dick Penner. He told us how the Lord impressed upon him to visit Jim in the hospital a few days before he died. After a short visit, Dick offered to pray for Jim. Jim said, "I don't need your prayers." Dick asked Jim if he had pain. Jim said, "I am suffering day and night."

Dick said, "Jim, you are dying and going to hell, where suffering will be much worse, for ever and ever." There was silence for a brief period.

Then Jim raised his hand and took Dick's hand and said, "Pray for me." Dick prayed for Jim. Then Jim prayed, asking Jesus to forgive him for all his sins, and to save him. As I heard Dick speak, what a joy filled my heart, that Dick had obeyed the Lord, and now Jim was safe with Jesus in Heaven. Praise the Lord!

February 7th. - I flew back to West Palm Beach, Florida, where our motorhome was.

February 9th. - Tyyne and I drove our motorhome from Lake Worth to Bradenton and to St. Petersburg. We visited Jim Montgomery who lived in a mobile home park in Clearwater.

February 11th. - I preached in the Assembly of God church in Seminole in the morning service. Rev. Hollingsworth is pastor.

February 12th. - 20th. - Attended the meetings at Christian Retreat, Bradenton, Florida. I preached in the morning service February 20th.

March 7th., 1979 - Miami. I shared on the talk show on TV channel 45, Lester Sumrall's station.

March 9th.- Received documents from Atco Company in Montreal for the two units they promised to build for a church at Wakeham Bay. Everything was changed in the documents to what we had agreed on.

March 10th.- Sunday. I preached in the Lake Worth Finnish Pentecostal church. When I gave the altar call, one lady came for salvation and six came for prayer and healing.

March 12th. - I phoned our bank to stop payment on my cheque to Atco Company.

March 14th. - Made reservations to fly to Montreal.

March 17th. - A few of our friends came to visit us in our motorhome. Had a good time of fellowship. I flew from the Fort Lauderdale airport to Toronto.

March 18th. - Sunday - my sister Cora and I attended Calvary Church.

March 19th. - Eric Lawton of Lawton Motors in Newmarket, offered me the use of one of his cars. I travelled to many different companies about building two units to use as a church in Wakeham Bay. I was informed that Bendix had a plant at St. Jerome, north of Montreal, who would build these units.

March 20th. - I drove from Exeter, Ontario to St. Jerome, Quebec.

March 21st. - Met with the manager of the Bendix Company and went over the plans for the two units. We agreed on a price. I wrote out a cheque for a deposit. I had a good talk with him about the Lord. Although he was Catholic, he appreciated our discussion. I drove to Atco in Montreal, cancelled my order, and got my deposit cheque back. I drove to Toronto.

March 22nd. - I returned the car to Lawton Brothers in Newmarket. I went by bus and subway to my sister Cora's place in Toronto.

March 23rd. - I took a street car, to subway, to a bus to Toronto Airport. Flew to Fort Lauderdale and arrived back at our motorhome in Lake Worth.

March 24th. - Returned to Cape Coral, Florida with our motorhome.

March 30th. - Drove to Christian Retreat, Bradenton. I preached in the AM service. We are starting our journey back to Ontario.

April 3rd., 1979 - In Cleveland, Tennessee, I shared in two sessions in Norvel Hayes Bible School. Also preached in the evening service in church. Some Canadians are students in the Bible School.

April 8th. - South Bend, Indiana. Attended Lester Sumrall's Sunday School and morning service. I preached in the evening service. A good offering was given for missionary work in the Canadian Arctic.

April 11th. - Drove to Wheaton, Illinois. Visited Paul Robinson, who accepted me as a student to learn to fly at the Moody Bible Institute in Chicago in January, 1950.

April 12th. - Near Gary, Indiana. I spoke at a women's meeting at "New Covenant" at Ramada Inn. A large crowd attended. When I gave the altar call, one elderly lady, sitting away back, was the first to come for salvation. I was told that this lady had attended these meetings for a long time, and the Christians had faithfully prayed for her salvation. Now they rejoiced as she made her commitment to Jesus.

April 13th. - Bernice Vista had made arrangements for me to speak to another group named the "Gathering". God blessed in this service, as a few more made commitments to Jesus.

April 15th. - Sunday.- Portage, Indiana. I was asked to speak at both AM and PM services. A very good crowd attended and many came forward for prayer.

April 16th. - One of the Christian ladies took me to a school where I shared with the students and showed slides of the Inuit. Tonight I shared at a Bible School.

April 17th. - Bernice Vista took me to the TV station Ch. 38 in Chicago, where I was on the talk show and shared some of my experiences of flying in the Canadian Arctic.

April 19th. - We drove our motorhome to the Lady Canterbury Inn, where I spoke in a Woman's Aglow meeting. Approximately 75 women were present. Had a good time of prayer for many different ailments and hurts.

April 20th. - We drove to Ottawa to Bill Prankard's. A member, Barry Armstrong, took us to his home, where we parked the motorhome.

April 26th. - Barry loaned me his car tp drive to St. Jerome to check on the two units for the church at Wakeham Bay. Everything proceeding well. Units will be ready for shipping.

I shared at Bill Prankard's meeting in a school auditorium this evening.

April 27th. - We drove the motorhome to Cornwall. I preached and showed Inuit slides in the Assembly church. A good crowd attended and God blessed.

April 28th. - I shared at the Full Gospel Business Men's breakfast. About 150 were in attendance. Many came forward for prayer, some for salvation, others for the baptism of the Holy Spirit, others for healing. We had a precious time in the presence of the Lord.

April 29th. - Long Sault, Ontario. I spoke to the Sunday School children in open session. I preached in the PM service of the Pentecostal church. God touched many hearts as His Word went forth.

May 4th., 1979 - I shared in the Sarnia Full Gospel Business Men's Fellowship meeting. Had a good time of prayer after the meeting.

May 5th. - Niagara-on-the-Lake. I spoke to a large Mennonite group in the Prince of Wales hotel. About 100 attended. They wanted to hear more about the Baptism of the Holy Spirit. A good time of discussion followed.

May 6th. - Sunday - I preached in the Full Gospel Church in Oil Springs, Ontario. This is a good missionary church and they have helped us financially with the Harvest Field missionary work.

May 7th. - We drove to Sarnia to visit Jim and Lena White. They asked me to share in a meeting in a nursing home. We had a precious time together around the Word of God.

May 8th. to 11th. Attended a Full Gospel Conference in the Travel Lodge in Sarnia, Ontario. I shared in the afternoon session on May 10th.

May 13th. - Sarnia - at the "Wings of Faith" Church. I shared in the Sunday School open session. The pastor asked me to preach in the AM service, and also in the evening service. I showed slides after the evening service of the Arctic work. A very good missionary offering was given for the work.

May 15th. - Tyyne and I flew from Toronto to Calgary to visit our youngest son David, his wife Shirley, and daughter Shelley.

May 20th. - I preached to a large crowd in John Lucas' church here in Calgary. Many responded to the altar call.

May 22nd. - Tyyne and I flew back to Toronto where we had left our motorhome.

May 23rd. - We met with Kayy Gordon, a missionary working in the Western Canadian Arctic, doing a great work.

May 25th. - Drove from Toronto to St. Jerome, Quebec to check on the two units Bendix is building. All is going well. Returned to Toronto.

May 26th. - Travelled north to Kirkland Lake to visit Glen and Grace Adams, who pastor the Pentecostal Assembly here.

May 27th. - Sunday - I shared in the morning worship service, a good crowd in attendance.

May 28th. - We returned to South Porcupine, to a large quantity of mail to be answered.

June 6th to June 21st., 1979 - Worked on the plane. Inspection on engine, fuselage and wings. Did some repair work.

Chapter 5

Another Missionary Trip

July 3rd., 1979 - In Austin's 748 plane. We flew north, stopping at Kapuskasing to take on a full load of groceries and other supplies. Refuelled at LG2. Flew on to Frobisher Bay, refuelled again. Unloaded about 6000 lbs. at Pangnirtung, then at Broughton Island and Clyde River.

July 4th. - Arrived at my destination of Pond Inlet. The sun shines day and night here. The Inuit sleeps when he is sleepy, he eats when he is hungry - rather than go by the clock.

July 5th. to 7th. - I am staying with the Anglican minister, Laurie Dexter. I visited quite a few homes and gave out gospel literature. A large Hercules plane came in and unloaded a large truck. Folk here are interested to know more about the Full Gospel message.

July 8th. - Sunday. Laurie asked me to speak to the teenagers and young adults in Sunday School. Also in the morning service of worship. Again at the 3 o'clock English service, and the 7 PM Inuit service, which was interpreted. God blessed as about 20 came forward for prayer.

July 9th. - The Inuits wanted a Bible Study, so we gathered in Charlie's home, a fine Christian Inuit family. The Word was made alive as we studied together.

July 10th. - Heavy fog all day, but Austin's 748 arrived and we flew south, stopping at all the settlements to Frobisher Bay.

July 11th. - After refuelling at Frobisher Bay, we flew non-stop to Timmins. Arrived home safe and sound.

July 26th. - A phone call from the Montreal Shipping Company said that our units ought to be at the harbour in a few days time, to be loaded on board the ship to Wakeham Bay. Tyyne and I packed things in our motorhome and started our trip south. Travelled as far as North Bay.

July 27th. - We drove to Ottawa. Visited a few friends.

July 28th. - Lea Pinet asked us to bring the motorhome to her place. We shopped for groceries and supplies.

July 29th. - Sunday - We attended Woodville Pentecostal church for the morning service. Tyyne and I drove to the Bendix plant at St. Jerome, Quebec.

July 30th. Both units are ready to be hauled to the Montreal Harbor. The Bendix plant will deliver them. Tyyne and I drove our motorhome to the Chimo shipping company at the harbor. After paying Bendix $20,000 for the two units, I made arrangements to ship them to Wakeham Bay. We drove to Walter Miller's home in Verdun where we parked the motorhome.

July 31st. - Flew from Dorval Airport in Nordair's 737 to Fort Chimo. John Recht invited me to stay in their home. Had a good Bible Study and prayer meeting here.

August 1st. - I got up at 5:45 AM. John took me to the airport. In Air Inuit's Twin Otter plane, we landed at Leaf Bay, Aupaluk, Payne Bay and Wakeham Bay. At each village I got out and distributed gospel literature to the people who came to meet the plane. Had turbulent winds and heavy rain squalls as we flew north.

August 2nd., 1979 - At Wakeham Bay, Quebec, on the south shore of Hudson Strait. I visited some families. Had a good Bible Study in an elderly Inuit man's home. The teaching was on, "What does God expect of us."

August 3rd. - We got the big Caterpillar bulldozer and levelled the site to put the two units on. Another good service - more people attended - Bible Study and prayer. These Inuit people are so sincere, as they worship the Lord.

August 4th. - The Co-Op supply ship arrived from Montreal - finished unloading with barges, as the ship is anchored quite a distance from shore. Another good evening service.

August 5th. - Sunday - Here at Wakeham Bay, the people are excited about getting a church building soon. We had a very good AM service in a home. A bigger crowd packed in for the evening service which was broadcast over the local radio station. God is doing a great work in hearts and lives.

August 6th. - Up at 3:45 AM. Ship arrived this morning. It came at 6:45 AM and anchored off shore. With the use of a tug and two barges, the ship was unloaded by 9:10 PM and our two units were on shore, above the high tide mark. Praise the Lord! The folk wanted another Bible study tonight which we finished at 11:20 PM. They appreciated it so much.

August 7th. A Quebec government man inspected our church site and suggested to us to move 30' over. We got the bulldozer and prepared the site - to everyone's satisfaction. We hauled the unit on site. A good crowd attended our evening service, which closed at 11:20 PM.

August 8th. - I had phoned Wilf and Ellen Remus at Palmer Rapids, Ontario and asked them to come and help us put these two units together and ready for services. They arrived on the Twin Otter plane at 3 PM today. It was a joy to see them. It rained most of the day. Our evening service started at 7 till 9:35 PM: a good time of rejoicing. Wilf is a hard worker and we appreciate him coming to help us.

August 9th. - Up at 6 AM. Wilf, Joseph the pastor, Mark Tetiluk, a hard working Inuit, and I, moved the second unit into place. I had sent up some 8" X10" X 12' timbers on the ship. We placed them under the two units and took off the sets of wheels.

Another good Bible Study. The Christian women brought us all the food and drink we needed. Ellen Remus was a great help to keep us refuelled.

August 10th. - Up at 6 AM. Worked on the units, jacking them over to form one building of 24' X 48'. We worked till 9:40 PM, dead tired, supper at 10 PM. No meeting.

August 11th. - Saturday. Up at 6. Finished the job at 9 PM. Hooked up the electrical power. Work completed and the church looks great. Praise the Lord!

August 12th., - Sunday was a great day for our congregation here at Wakeham Bay. I had shipped up a lot of chairs and we held the Dedication Service for this church. The building was packed full with the village people. Tears of joy were shed, as our Christians thanked the Lord for answering their prayers.

August 13th. - We rested part of the day. Had a very good evening service. I spoke on the Baptism of the Holy Spirit. Eight received this experience.

August 14th. - The Twin Otter plane arrived and we flew out to Fort Chimo.

August 15th. - Some of the Inuits took us by canoe to "Old" Fort Chimo, a few miles down the river. Many musk-ok were fenced here to increase the herd. Had a good service tonight in one of the homes.

August 16th. - One of the Inuit men came to visit us this morning. He accepted Jesus as Savior. We flew to Montreal in Nordair's 737. After we had a good supper in our motorhome here, Wilf and Ellen Remus left to drive home to Palmer Rapids.

August 17th. - I drove to the Chimo Shipping Co., and was handed a shipping bill for $31,383.45 to deliver the two units to Wakeham Bay. After discussion, the bill was reduced $2500.00 to $28,883.45. I will say that's the first and last time I had units built and shipped north. I contacted an insurance company and took out an insurance policy on the church at Wakeham Bay. We drove our motorhome as far as Mattawa and spent the night.

August 18th. - Up at 3:30 AM. Drove till 6 AM, stopped for breakfast. Drove to Kirkland Lake. Visited Glen and Grace, then drove to South Porcupine and home. Mission accomplished. All thanks and glory and honor to Jesus!

August 23rd. - Appalled by the boat people tragedy, a group of us gathered in the South Porcupine Pentecostal Church basement, and agreed to rescue some of them. For income tax purposes, we would give receipts under the Harvest Field banner. Ron Walker agreed to be the secretary treasurer.

August 24th. - Ron Walker and I went to the bank and opened a new account for the boat people, as a good size offering was taken last night.

August 30th. - Noah Isaac phoned from Sugluk, Quebec on the Hudson Strait, for me to come up for meetings. Qolingo Tookalak phoned from Povungnituk for me to come up.

September 1st., 1979 - I performed a wedding for a couple in the Timmins Salvation Army church.

September 5th. - Ron Walker and I signed papers in the Immigration office in Timmins, that we would be responsible for a group of Vietnamese boat people for one year. This is for living quarters, food and clothing - total expenses.

September 6th. - Up at 3 AM. I flew to Cape Dorset on Baffin Island where we built the church last year. Udjualuk met me at the airport. Very good evening service in the new church. Four adults came forward for salvation.

September 7th. - I prepared documents for two weddings to take place tomorrow. Good evening Bible Study in our Full Gospel Church.

September 8th. - Saturday - I performed two weddings this morning in our church. Udjualuk and I flew to Sugluk. Had a very good service in Noah Isaac's home. Retired at 11:45 PM.

September 9th. - Sunday in Sugluk. Good service this morning with a good crowd attending in Noah Isaac's home. Visited a few families in the afternoon. Another bigger service this evening from 6 PM to 1:10 Monday morning. God is moving by His Holy Spirit.

September 10th. - Visited a few families. Evening Bible Study on "Gifts of the Spirit", till midnight. Very interesting teaching.

September 11th. - Another good Bible Study all morning till plane time. Udjualuk and I flew to Povungnituk. Bible teaching this evening on giving God top priority in our lives, to do His will and not our own.

September 12th. - In Qolingo Tookalak's home. Another good Bible Study. God blessed us in a wonderful way and touched hearts. Udjualuk and I flew to Port Harrison. We stayed in John Williams' home. Visited a few families and the Anglican minister.

September 15th. - Saturday - Snowing and blowing all day. Had a good talk with John Williams' wife. She accepted Jesus. Had a good Bible Study.

September 16th. - We flew to Great Whale River. Four accepted Jesus in our evening service in Appliee Napartuk's home. The people here want a Full Gospel Church.

September 17th. - Austin's 748 plane arrived and I flew out to Timmins and home.

Chapter 6

The Boat People

Matthew 7:12 Jesus said: "Therefore all things whatsoever ye would that men should do to you, do ye even so to them: for this is the law and the prophets."

October 3rd., 1979 - I had lengthy interviews with the TV station people, also Timmins Radio, and the Daily Newspaper, regarding the Vietnamese Boat People. I had a good reception with each one and they were all in favor with what we are doing.

October 5th. - Carl Haacke and I borrowed Ron Tryon's truck and collected beds, mattresses, kitchen table, chairs and clothing for the Boat People who would arrive soon.

October 8th. - Eric Inkilainen donated a good fridge and electric stove.

October 13th. - Russel and Greta Thom donated a good washing machine.

October 15th. - We collected all these items, as well as pots, pans, dishes and bedding for the Boat People.

October 25th. - Cecil and Ethel Stearns gave a good vacuum cleaner. Immigration office phoned. We were told that our request for a Vietnamese couple with possibly two or three children, could not be filled. But we were asked if we would accept a young man and his sister and two other men instead. I believe all these were between twenty and twenty five years old.

We called for a meeting of supporters and discussed this matter. We all agreed that we should accept them. We therefore notified the Immigration authorities of our decision. We were advised that it may take up to two weeks before these young people would arrive.

We rented an upstairs apartment on the corner of Crawford St. and Golden Ave. in South Porcupine for these boat people. We made arrangements for them to attend classes to learn the English language. These classes would last all winter till late in the spring.

It was nearing our time to leave for Florida. We knew that Ron Walker, Carl Haacke and other supporters would look after the boat people well when they would arrive.

I found out later that the first group of Boat people came from Laos, landed in Canada at Montreal on February 7th., 1980 and arrived in Timmins on February 10th. They were a lady and her brother, Toumkham and Khantanh Bounprasueth, and two other young men: Bounlert Phomsouvanh and Oudone Thepkasone.

October 29th. - Tyyne, Dan and I started on our trip to Florida. We shared and preached in many different churches and groups as we travelled south in our motorhome. We found many open doors to have fellowship both in Canada and in the United States. During the winter months we travelled extensively around the State of Florida. I was guest on a few TV talk shows in Miami and in Clearwater, Florida. I was also guest speaker at a number of the Full Gospel Business Men's Fellowship meetings.

In one of the Sebring, Florida churches, a big revival meeting was planned. We were asked if we would stay to visit house to house along with other couples. So for two weeks before the revival meetings, Tyyne and I knocked on doors and visited in many homes. We met many fine people. Some young married couples had no Bible, so we were able to get one and present it to them as a gift. This happened quite a few times. We also met some Jewish people, and it was a delight to share with them the good news of another Jew, born of Mary in the city of Bethlehem, Jesus, the Son of God.

A number of the people visited, were very open to the claims of Christ and accepted Jesus right there and then.

While in Cape Coral, we had a wonderful time of fellowship with our oldest daughter Rose and her husband Bob Harmer. We had many good swims in their large swimming pool.

March 31st., 1980 - We left Cape Coral and journeyed northward. We were able to keep our schedule of meetings on time, and we saw quite a few people saved and healed in the meetings.

We crossed the Canadian border at Windsor, Ontario on April 15th., 1980 at 3 PM. It always feels good to be back in Canada.

From April 15th to May 30th., 1980 we travelled in Southern Ontario right across to Ottawa, in meetings and sharing what God is doing in the Canadian Arctic. I showed my Arctic slides to many congregations. Again, God blessed and souls were saved.

We had rented out our home in South Porcupine to tenants for the winter months. They moved out on May 30th. and we moved in.

June 1st., 1980 - Sunday - Minus 3 below zero C. It was so good to see the five Boat people who were refugees from Laos. They were all well taken care of and learning English. Ron Walker and Carl Haacke did a wonderful job taking care of them. All five of them accompanied us to the services in the

Pentecostal church.

June 2nd. - I took one of the Boat people men, Bert (we shortened his first name about 1/2 of it's length, but left his last name as is) Phomsouvanh, to Lloyd Richards Cartage and Haulage Company, and he started to work.

June 3rd. and 4th. - Dan and I worked on the plane, and I flew it from Morris Hibbards' where we had left it for the winter, to South Porcupine Lake.

June 6th. - Took some Boat people shopping for clothing and groceries.

June 8th. - Minus 2 degrees C. to plus 2. The ground is covered with snow. Boat people go to all the church services.

June 9th. - 10th. - Office work. Took the Boat people to English classes; shopped for both ourselves and the Boat people.

June 11th. - 14th. - Plenty of work in the office and with the Boat people.

June 16th. - Word from the north is that lots of ice covers all the lakes and bays. I purchased a plane ticket and flew to Toronto and then to Montreal.

June 17th. - I flew north to Fort Chimo in Nordair's 737 jet. I checked to see about renting the High School auditorium for the Bill Prankard meetings next month. Quite a few Inuit people gathered in Hans' home and we had a good Bible Study and time of prayer. Returned at 9:05 PM from the Chimo River where I baptized Mrs. Shelly Recht in water. There were snow banks on the shore and the water was icy cold. Last year I baptized Bro. Recht at the same place.

June 18th. - Plane flights cancelled on account of weather. I visited homes and we had another good Bible Study at Hans'.

June 19th. - Still here in Fort Chimo. Arrangements were finalized for the Bill Prankard meetings next month. Visited a few homes and gave out gospel literature.

June 20th. - Made reservations with a local pilot who has a small twin engine plane, to fly the Bill Prankard party to Cape Dorset on Baffin Island, then to Wakeham Bay for services, and return to Fort Chimo. That's for next month.

June 21st. - Weather has cleared. I purchased my ticket on Air Inuit's Twin Otter plane to Payne Bay. We stopped at Leaf Bay and Aupaluk enroute. A good crowd gathered for the evening service. One man accepted Jesus as Savior.

June 22nd. - Sunday. Had a good Bible Study in the home where I am staying this morning. Then we met in another home for an afternoon service. We attended the Anglican Church evening service.

June 23rd. - Two young ladies, I believe around 18 years old, came to visit - both of them accepted Jesus. Others came for prayer and counselling. The plane arrived and I flew on to Quaqtaq. A good crowd gathered for the evening service which started at 8 PM and lasted until midnight. God blessed and many hearts were touched by the power of God.

June 24th. - Quaqtaq This morning a fine young man came in to talk about salvation. After explaining the way and reading many scriptures, with tears in his eyes, he prayed and received Jesus as Saviour. A group of Christian Inuit men came over to discuss plans to build a small building here for a church. Since the village is small and our Christians are small in number, they suggested a building 24' X 36'. They all said it was too large but later agreed to that size. I promised to send all the material up by ship from Montreal. Another great service in Pootalook's home, from 7 PM to 11 PM. Many came forward for prayer.

June 25th. - I flew on to Wakeham Bay. All the lakes and the Hudson Strait are solid ice. Many gathered in the new church building of last year, for a service. God touched many hearts. Some came forward for salvation, others to be stronger Christians. Six received the Baptism of the Holy Spirit.

June 26th. - I visited a few homes. Had a wonderful time of worship and a communion service from 7 PM to 9:15 PM. Yet the people hungered for more, so we had a Bible Study on the Second Coming of Christ from 9:30 PM to 12 midnight.

June 27th. The plane arrived and I flew to Sugluk. The landing strip is about six miles up river, which is open water in some places and solid ice in others. The men of the village had quite a time to get us out. They travelled by skidoo part of the way, pulling a sled with a big canoe on it. Then they had to leave the skidoo and come the rest of the way by canoe through broken ice, then to open water. It was late when we at last arrived at the village. Our Christians wanted a Bible Study immediately, which lasted till midnight.

June 28th. - I visited quite a few Inuit homes and gave out Gospel literature in the Inuit language. On our way to the air strip, we rode a skidoo pulling a sled with a large canoe on top. At last the driver said we cannot take the skidoo any further, as the ice was not safe. So we unloaded the canoe and pushed it for at least another mile on the ice. One of our men fell through the ice, but he was wearing waterproof clothing and waist waders. For the last two miles we were able to ride in the canoe, going between pans of ice. The plane arrived shortly after we got there and we flew south. A fine Inuit man was sitting beside me. I soon found out that he was interested in becoming a Christian. He accepted Jesus as his Savior. He disembarked at Akulivik and we flew on to Povungnituk. We gathered in one of the Inuit homes and had a good Bible

Study till 11:30 PM.

June 29th. - Sunday. 8:30 AM. Here in Qolingo's home in Povungnituk. The people wanted another Bible teaching this forenoon. God blessed and the people's questions were answered from the Word. We checked some fish nets this afternoon. Many Inuits gathered in another larger home for our evening Bible Study which ended at midnight.

June 30th. - Here at Povungnituk. I got up at 6:15 AM. The plane took off at 8:15 AM. We flew to Port Harrison, Belcher Islands and to Great Whale River. I gave out gospel literature in the Inuit language in the different settlements. Also talked to a number of Inuit who appeared interested in the gospel. I stayed at Appliee Napartuk's home where many people gathered in and we had a wonderful time of study around the Word of God. A number requested prayer for healing, some for deliverance from bad habits, etc.

July 1st., 1980 - At Great Whale River on the Hudson Bay east coast. Had good discussions with a few Inuit this morning. Flew in Austin's 748 turbo jet to Fort George, Paint Hills, Eastmain, Rupert's House, Moosonee and on to Timmins and home, where a lot of work was waiting for me.

July 3rd. - Had a Harvest Field Boat People meeting to discuss our financial status and future plans.

Jesus said in Luke 19:13, "Occupy till I come."

July 5th. - Prepared motorhome for trip to Montreal to purchase materials and supplies.

July 6th. - Sunday. We attended Sunday School and morning service. Finished packing things in the motorhome. Drove south to North Bay. Stopped for the night.

July 7th. - Left early this morning and drove to Ottawa. Visited some friends and continued about halfway to Montreal. We parked at a gas station for the night.

July 8th. - Continued our trip to Montreal. The lumber supply company had moved north of Montreal. We drove there and figured out all the supplies needed for the Quaqtaq Church as well as a small shipment to Wakeham Bay.

July 9th.- 15th. - We bundled up 2 X 4's, 2 X 6's, 2 X 8's and also plywood. Made up crates 4' wide and 8' long: packed in insulation, small items, etc. We hauled three truckloads to the Montreal Harbor, where each crate and bundle were measured and weighed. The shipping bill was figured out and I paid for all the material and shipping.

July 16th. - Drove north; visited in Pembroke, New Liskeard, Kirkland Lake and home. Mission accomplished.

July 17th. - 25th. - Worked with the Laotian Boat people.

Worked in our office answering letters and bringing our financial book up to date. We print and send out some 400 Harvest
Field Newsletters each month.

July 26th. - Since we are not using our 185 Cessna plane,
our Board of Directors advised to sell it. Four men flew to
Timmins airport from Quebec City in a small twin engine plane.
Our plane was sold to them. Two of the men flew the 185
Cessna to Quebec City and the other two flew the twin back.

July 28th. - I purchased plane tickets for Jim and Lena White
of Sarnia, and myself to fly to Cape Dorset and return.

July 30th. - Jim and Lena arrived by car from Sarnia. We
packed up for the flight north.

July 31st. - Up at 4 AM. Jim and Lena White and I flew from
Timmins to Cape Dorset. The church we built in 1978 was
packed full for the evening service. Udjualuk the pastor is
doing a great job of shepherding this flock. Brother and Sister
White brought up an overhead projector for the church. After
I brought the message from the Word, I gave the altar call.
Many Inuit came forward for prayer: some for salvation, oth-
ers for healing and others to become stronger Christians.

August 1st., 1980 - Five degrees C. Made arrangements to
hold a baptismal service tomorrow. The Christians love to sing
the gospel choruses, with upraised hands, and some with
tears of joy flowing down their cheeks. Tonight's service
ended at 11 PM.

August 2nd. - Saturday. A cold morning. Jim and Lena conducted children's church at 2 o'clock. A large crowd gathered
at the small lake behind the village. We put up a small tent to
change in. A couple had come from Ivugivik: Lucassie and
Louisa Kanarjuak, to be baptized, along with others from the
congregation here. It was a great time of rejoicing.

Again the church was packed full for the evening service. I
preached on the subject of the Baptism of the Holy Spirit.
Acts 2:38-39, Acts 2:1-4. A great time of prayer followed. Six
of our Inuit Christians testified that now they have been baptized in the Holy Spirit.

August 3rd. - Sunday. A big crowd gathered in for the morning worship. Jim and Lena White conducted Sunday School
for the children this afternoon. Bro. Jim preached in the
evening service to a full church, followed by a young people's
meeting 9:15 PM to 10:30 PM.

August 4th. - I spoke to more than 60 children who gathered in for children's church this afternoon. Another good
crowd attended the evening service, My subject was "The
Rapture". Many came forward for a time of prayer.

August 5th. - Visited a number of homes today. Prayed for
some sick folk. Two men built a tank to be used for baptism. It

was filled with water this afternoon. In the evening service, we baptized two more in water. Then after we dismissed the service, one man came rushing in and said he wanted to be saved and baptized too. So we also baptized him in water.

August 6th. - Rev. Stringer of the Pentecostal Church in Frobisher Bay, had heard of the remarkable move of God here at Cape Dorset. He phoned and asked us to come and have a service for him. I purchased two plane tickets for Udjualuk and myself and we flew to Frobisher Bay. On our arrival Rev. Stringer informed us that he had no people to come for a meeting. He apologized that no meeting was possible, since he had requested us to come.

August 7th. - I purchased two tickets for Udjualuk and I to fly to Pond Inlet on the northern coast of Baffin Island. We took off at 8:15 AM and flew to Broughton Island, Clyde River, then to Pond Inlet. We had a very good service in Caleb Ootova's home. I spoke on the Baptism of the Holy Spirit. Six Inuit testified they have now received the Baptism. One Inuit man accepted Jesus as his Savior.

August 8th. - Visited quite a few homes today. Had Bible reading and prayer with them. Evening service in Caleb's home. One young man requested prayer as he had given his life over to Satan and was involved in alcohol and drugs. He accepted Jesus.

August 9th. - Caleb took Udjualuk and I in his speedboat about 40 miles down the coast westward toward his camp. One of our Canadian icebreakers was unloading drums of oil by helicopter to be used in an experiment if an oil spill would happen and how they would contain it. One of the men on the icebreaker took us on a tour of the ship and we had tea with them. Back in Pond Inlet, a greater crowd gathered for the evening service. I spoke on "Faith". The people appreciated the Bible teaching and asked many questions.

August 10th. - Pond Inlet, N.W.T. - Sunday. We attended the morning service in the Anglican Church. I was asked to come and speak in the two o'clock young people's meeting. Nine of the young Inuit came forward for salvation. Four of the young people came to Caleb's house after, and they too accepted Jesus. I also preached in the evening service in the Anglican Church and a good number came forward for salvation, some with tears of repentance, as they called on the Lord to save them.

August 11th. - Caleb asked us to visit his brother in Clyde River, so Udjualuk and I flew there and had a good visit with them. We also visited two families and the Anglican minister.

August 12th. - Clyde River. Bethuel Ootova mentioned how he had prayed that God would send somebody to teach him about the Holy Spirit. God answered his prayer. Another woman told how she had prayed for weeks, that God would send somebody to pray for her healing. Again, God answered her prayer. Tonight we had a good meeting in this home. We prayed for quite a few for salvation, healing and the Baptism of the Holy Spirit.

August 13th. - Clyde River. Met quite a number of Inuit who are interested in the gospel. I gave out New Testaments and gospel literature. It was the regular weekly Anglican service and we attended the Anglican Church.

August 14th. - Bill Prankard's office phoned, requesting Udjualuk to fly to Ottawa. So we had to change our plans, and I flew on alone to Broughton Island. The Anglican minister had phoned asking me to stop there to visit him. Jonah, the Anglican minister, met me at the airstrip and said I would be staying in his home. We had a good visit, Bible Study and prayer this evening.

August 15th. - Broughton Island, in Rev. Jonah Alooloo's home. Had another good Bible Study. I visited in a few homes and found people who were really interested in the Full Gospel message. Prayed for a number of people.

August 16th. - Broughton Island on the east coast of Baffin Island. A helicopter flew in to get supplies for the men on an oil rig about 80 miles offshore toward Greenland. I gave out New Testaments in English and Inuit languages.

August 17th. - Sunday. I attended Jonah's services in the Anglican Church. Met Mark, a fine Inuit man who was interested. He accepted Jesus. Also prayed with a number of people with various needs.

August 18th. - At Broughton Island. I visited a schoolteacher and a couple working for First Air Airways. I flew to Frobisher Bay. Got a room at the Inuit Inn. I was tired.

August 19th. - Frobisher Bay. I met Joe Little from South Porcupine, Ontario. He is working up here now. I met many Inuit and I gave out gospel literature and had good talks with some. Austin Airway's plane arrived and we took off just before midnight.

August 20th. - Flying south - arrived at Timmins airport at 5:30 AM. Worked in office. Checked Laotian Boat people. They need another apartment. I rented a good apartment on 103 Moore St., South Porcupine, and we moved them there.

August 21st. - I had the Hydro and phone connected at 103 Moore Street. Paid the insurance on the church buildings at Cape Dorset, Wakeham Bay and Quaqtaq. Office work.

August 24th. - Sunday. I preached in the morning service in the South Porcupine Pentecostal church. Three came forward for salvation, others for healing. I preached in the evening service in the Finnish Pentecostal church and showed my slides of the Arctic.

August 26th. - I contacted the Immigration office about the Laotian Boat People, who asked me to find work for them. Contacted many companies, garages, saw mills, gold mines, till October 12th.

Chapter 7

More Challenges

Genesis 12:9 "Abram journeyed south"

October 13th.,1980 - 4 degrees below zero C., ground covered with snow. We drove south in our motorhome and had many meetings enroute. Arrived in Cape Coral, Florida, November 13th. 82 degrees F. Our mail and Harvest Field mail forwarded to us here from South Porcupine.

March 21st., - 1981. We've had a busy winter here in Florida. Temperatures were warm and we usually only wore shorts around home. Had good services in many different churches and groups. God blessed and souls were saved. Now it's time to leave the sunny south and travel north.

March 25th. - At Orlando, Florida, we attended the large "Jesus 81" meetings. Approximately 35,000 people here.

April 6th., 1981 - We crossed the border at Windsor.

April 12th. - Sunday. We attended the Sunday School and morning service at the Pentecostal Church where Glen and Grace are pastor. We drove north to South Porcupine and home in the afternoon.

April 14th. - 18 degrees below zero C., snow and blowing. Why didn't we stay in Florida a little longer?

April 18th. - We had sold our plane last year, because we were not using it enough, and I had flown many trips to the Arctic by commercial plane. But today Rick Oliver phoned from Portland, Oregon, U.S.A., that he had heard a lot about our missionary work, and he wanted to work with us. He is not only a pilot but also an instructor as well as a helicopter pilot. He advised us to buy another plane, and he would fly it in extensive missionary work all through the Eastern Arctic. He said he definitely felt the call of God to this work. Rick said that he was single and had no obligations or debts; furthermore he had an income and would require no pay - as long as we could provide the missionary plane. In fact, he knew of a good plane for sale in Edmonton and that he would meet me there. I called a Harvest Field Directors meeting and agreed to go ahead with plans.

April 20th. - 20 degrees below zero C. Made reservations to fly to Edmonton.

May 5th. - 6th., 1981 - Drove from South Porcupine. Visited at North Bay, Gooderham and arrived in Toronto.

May 7th. - I flew to Edmonton. Met Rick Oliver at the airport. We checked over the 185 Cessna. We flew it around with Rick as pilot as he would be the one flying in the Arctic. Rick was not satisfied with the plane's performance and decided we should not buy it. He said there was another one in Calgary, so we decided to go and see it.

May 8th. - Rick had driven from Portland, Oregon with his parents in their car. So we all left Edmonton and travelled south to Calgary. The plane here in Calgary was not what we needed. Rick and his parents drove back to Portland disappointed.

May 9th. - I flew to Winnipeg. A Christian brother met me at the airport and drove me to Steinbach to the Innus' home. He is in the airplane business and has three crop spraying planes which he and two other pilots fly all over Manitoba spraying crops.

May 10th. - Sunday. We attended the Steinbach Full Gospel Church at the 8:30 AM service, also the 10 AM Sunday School and the second morning service at 11 AM. I was asked to share in the evening service. We prayed for quite a few after the evening service. Glen Foresberg is pastor.

May 11th. - The Innus told me of a 185 Cessna plane for sale in Winnipeg. Ike phoned the owner to fly the plane over to Steinbach. I flew the plane and Ike and I checked it all over and decided to buy it for $51,500.00. I paid a small deposit on it, with the agreement that the balance would be paid in about two weeks. The plane was left in Ike's care at Steinbach.

May 13th. - I am back in Toronto where I left my car. Very cool weather.

May 14th. - Drove north to South Porcupine.

May 15th. - 19th. - Worked in office. Printed 525 of our Harvest Field newsletters and mailed them out. Sent a certified cheque to Winnipeg of $46,500.00, the balance owing on the plane.

May 20th. - I phoned Rick Oliver to meet me in Winnipeg. I started the drive with my car from South Porcupine. Left at 5:45 AM, drove west to Wawa, Thunder Bay, Fort Francis and to Emo, Ontario, where I stopped for the night.

May 21st. - Left Emo and drove across the U.S. border into Minnesota and north up to Steinback, Manitoba. The 185 Cessna, CGVXV, looked beautiful.

May 22nd. I drove into Winnipeg to transfer the plane to Harvest Field Inc. I took out insurance on the plane and a total of five passengers, which cost $4,863.00 per year.

May 23rd. - Had a meeting with Pastor Glen Foresberg and board members, who wanted to have a part in this missionary work in the Canadian Arctic.

May 24th. - Sunday, at Steinbach, Manitoba. The Innus and I

attended morning worship. I preached in the evening service. Four came forward to receive Jesus as Savior.

May 25th. - I drove to Winnipeg airport and met Rick Oliver, who arrived after a very late flight from Portland, Oregon.

May 26th. - Rick and I had a meeting with the pastor and board members of the Full Gospel Church. After the pastor and board members asked Rick many questions about his background, they decided not to have a part in this project.

May 27th. - Rick returned to Portland and I travelled east as far as Marathon, where I stopped at a motel - $27.00 per night. I received word a few weeks later that Rick was called to Africa to train helicopter pilots. He was killed, hit by a propeller.

May 28th. - After leaving Marathon, I picked up a hitchhiker. Had a good talk with him. He accepted the Lord. Arrived safely home in South Porcupine.

May 29th. - June 2nd. - Worked in office. Balanced books, answered many letters. Made reservations to fly to the Arctic.

June 3rd., 1981 - Flew from Timmins Airport to Toronto and on to Montreal.

June 4th. - Flew north to Fort Chimo. Visited a few families. Had Bible reading and prayed for a few sick Inuit.

June 5th. - Was supposed to fly to Payne Bay but it's snowing and blowing so no flying today. Visited more homes till late tonight.

June 6th. - Weather not too good but we flew to Payne Bay. Snow blizzard. Many Inuit came to the home where I am staying. Had a very good Bible teaching all evening.

June 7th. - Sunday. Real winter weather, snowing and cold. We had a good morning service in Peter's home where I am staying. Many gathered in for our evening service. Nine Inuit came forward and received Jesus.

June 9th. - Weather not too good but we flew to Quaqtaq where we built the church last year. A great crowd gathered in the new church for an evening service. Many came up for prayer, to be delivered of smoking, two received the Baptism of the Holy Spirit. Had good Bible discussion till 12 midnight.

June 10th. - Here at Quaqtaq - wintry weather. Plane arrived to fly to Wakeham Bay, my destination. We tried to land, but the weather was 0 0, so we flew on to Sugluk.I visited a few people, then attended the Anglican Church weekly service.

June 11th. - Sugluk on the Hudson Strait. I am staying in George's home. One Inuit man came to see me and inquired about salvation. He accepted Jesus. While I was walking toward the Hudsons Bay store, I met a young Inuit woman. She had attended our service on my last visit here but had not accepted Jesus. She accepted Jesus right there on the street. A very good service in Molley's home - good attendance. Many inquired about the Baptism of the Holy Spirit.

June 12th. - A few men came to discuss some questions. I showed them the answers found in the Bible. A good Bible Study this evening in one of the converts home. I appreciated the questions asked, as we discussed various topics.

June 13th. - Plane was supposed to come in, but bad weather and snow would not allow it. We waited at the landing strip. I had a good talk with three men at the airstrip about eternity.

June 14th. - Sunday. I phoned home, as I do every Sunday morning. Plane is supposed to come at 12:30 noon. We waited in vain. Had a good Bible Study on the "Second Coming of Christ" in our evening service. Noah's house was packed full of people. We prayed for seven Inuit, for salvation and healing.

June 15th. - Another service was requested for tonight at 7 PM. Three Inuit accepted Jesus.

June 16th. - Still no plane. Visited homes. Another good meeting tonight. God touched many hearts.

June 17th. - Snow blizzard all day - so why waste time! Had a good Bible Study in Noah's home this morning, also another one in the afternoon. More Inuits accepted Jesus.

June 18th. - Another Bible Study on our "Obedience to Christ". One elderly woman and one young married man accepted Jesus. Some Inuit hunters shot 14 whales. They distributed whale meat to all the families.

June 21st. - Sunday again. I phoned home. Good flying weather here but not at Great Whale nor at Povungnituk. So planes can't fly. Another good Bible Study. Noah's sister accepted Jesus, and Mark, an Inuit man, accepted Jesus too.

June 22nd. - Austin Airway's plane cannot come. But Air Inuit from Fort Chimo will come. I purchased my ticket to fly to Fort Chimo. Another good Bible Study was requested for tonight. Two young Inuit women accepted Jesus.

June 23rd. Air Inuit plane arrived. We flew from Sugluk to Fort Chimo and on to Montreal. Got a room at the Grand Hotel, $30.00.

June 24th. In Montreal - flew to Toronto. Changed planes. Flew to North Bay, then to Timmins. Tyyne came and got me. Home again, to lots of work.

June 25th. - July 3rd./81 - Worked in office. Matthew and his wife phoned me from Timmins Empire Hotel, that they had flown down from Ivugivik for me to baptize them in water.

July 5th., 1981 - Sunday. I went to Timmins and got Matthew and his Lydia, the two Inuits who flew down from Ivugivik to be baptized in water. We attended the AM service in the Pentecostal Church. Quite a nice group gathered at the far end of Porcupine Lake where there was a nice sandy beach. We had a nice service, then I baptized them both in water.

They wanted to fly back to Ivugivik immediately but we persuaded them to stay over for a couple day's holiday.

July 6th. - South Porcupine. Tyyne and I took Matthew and Lydia out fishing with boat and motor. They had an enjoyable time.

July 7th. - I took Matthew and Lydia from our home to the Timmins Airport. They flew north to Ivugivik.

July 16th. - I checked the weather up north. It appears good. Took off in Austin's 748 at 5:55 AM. Flew to Cape Dorset on Baffin Island. A good crowd gathered for Bible teaching. Prayer for quite a few Inuit.

July 17th. - Cape Dorset. Udjualuk and his wife Minnie returned home from a fishing trip. Another good service in the church.

July 18th. - Sunday. I preached in the morning service; had a good time of prayer. The people requested a service at 2:30 this afternoon. A larger crowd gathered and we had a precious time in the Presence of the Lord.

A bigger crowd attended the 7 PM service. When I gave the altar call, 12 or 13 came forward for prayer. One fine young married Inuit woman received Jesus as Savior.

July 20th. - I purchased tickets for Udjualuk and I to fly to Pond Inlet on the northern end of Baffin Island. We had a very good evening service and time of prayer here at Cape Dorset.

July 21st. - I visited one of the Inuit Christian's homes. Udjualuk and I flew to Frobisher Bay. People gathered in Mosesee's home. We had a good service and time of prayer.

July 22nd. - Frobisher Bay. Udjualuk and I flew north of the Arctic Circle to Pond Inlet. The Anglican minister asked me to stay in his home. His name is Jim Bell. The sun shines overhead day and night here at Pond inlet and all the settlements north of the Arctic Circle.

July 23rd. - Pond Inlet. I visited a few homes and shared the good news of Jesus. Had a good service in one of the Inuit homes and a time of prayer after.

July 24th. - I was reminded today of our $2.00 bill. On the back is a picture of Inuit seal hunting. I met one of those men here today. Five or six Inuit asked me to baptize them in water. A large crowd gathered at a small lake just above the village. A strong cold wind was blowing and I was cold even with my parka on. We put up a small tent. I was the first to take off all my winter clothing and just have a pair of trousers on and a shirt. I asked the Lord to help us, and I walked into the extremely cold water. After baptizing two of the candidates, I felt warm and could have baptized people all day long. This was the first water baptismal service by immersion ever here at Pond Inlet. We had another great service tonight in the same home as last night.

July 25th. - I visited a couple of homes. A 13 year old boy accepted Jesus as Saviour. The temperature was 0 degrees C. with snow flurries. The biggest crowd yet gathered in this large home for our evening service. Some of the men are out hunting narwhale, which has the long ivory tusk.

July 26th. - Sunday. We attended the Anglican Church morning service. I was asked to preach in the evening service here in the Anglican Church. A large crowd gathered and God blessed in the service. When I gave the altar call for those who wanted to be saved, eight Inuit responded and came forward for prayer. Also three others to re-dedicate their lives to Jesus.

July 27th. - Rev. Jim Bell, the Anglican minister, took my baggage to the airport. Udjualuk and I flew to Nanisivik which is northwest of Pond Inlet. We took a taxi the eighteen miles to Arctic Bay. A very large crowd gathered in the community hall for a service. The Anglican minister, Larry Dexter interpreted for me. God blessed and touched many hearts. We were invited to one of the Inuit's homes. Quite a few of the people followed us over. We had a second service. One man and his wife accepted Jesus.

July 28th. - Arctic Bay, N.W.T. A number of Inuit came to the home where I was staying. We had a good discussion on what the Bible teaches for one to live a Christian life. A taxi took us back to the airport at Nanisivik. We flew to Igloolik. Our Christians were glad to see us and asked for a meeting. Our Bible teaching ended after 1 AM.

July 29th. - Igloolik, N.W.T., an island off the northwest coast of Baffin Island, near the mainland. I visited a white lady reporter, also the Catholic priest: had prayer with both of them. A very good meeting held in Jake's house with a good attendance.

July 30th. - I visited a few homes. Many hunters are out hunting narwhale. They say the narwhale hide is the very best food in the world. Another good Bible Study in Jake's home, with a few people prayed for after service.

July 31st. - Igloolik, N.W.T. Another good day of visitation. I met some Inuit who were vitally interested in what the Bible says. A good number gathered in Jake's home and we had an interesting time of discussion.

August 1st., 1981 - Igloolik, N.W.T. A very fine young Catholic Inuit lady came over to the home where I was staying. She asked many questions which were bothering her. I told her not to believe anyone, minister or priest or myself, unless the answer was given and shown in the Bible. The plane arrived late. We flew to Hall's Beach, to Frobisher Bay and on to Fort Chimo.

August 2nd. - Sunday at Fort Chimo. I am staying in Brother Faucolt's home. Jacques and I attended the morning service in the Anglican Church. The supply ship had arrived this morning while we were in church. Jacques had to go immediately to help unload the supplies while the tide was high. He returned just after 2 PM as the tide was going out. He is a good cook, and he made a wonderful dinner for both of us, and also supper later on this evening. We had a wonderful time of Christian fellowship discussing the Word of God. The tide started to come in about 10 PM and he had to leave to unload the ship.

August 3rd. - Fort Chimo. Another great day of visitation sharing with a number of people on what the born again experience means. Jacque went to work at 7 AM and returned at 3:30 AM early Tuesday morning.

August 4th. - Tuesday. Up at 6 AM. I packed and rushed to the airport, bought a ticket to Wakeham Bay; flew there and conducted a business meeting of the church members. Joseph Nappaaluk was chosen as pastor for this congregation. The plane had flown on to Sugluk and returned. I was able to fly to Payne Bay. Here the one tire on the plane went flat. The pilot had to radio to Fort Chimo to bring another tire. While this was going on, the people here at Payne Bay requested a meeting. Quite a few gathered and we had a good time of fellowship, discussing the Word of God. Our meeting ended, the plane tire was replaced and we flew on to Fort Chimo. I stayed at Jacques place.

August 5th. - Fort Chimo. Up at 7 AM. Jacques had arrived home at 3:30 AM and had to return to work at 7:45 AM. Met a few men from Wakeham Bay and Sugluk. I flew to Montreal, stayed at the Airport Inn - $32.00.

August 6th. - Montreal - up at 6 AM. The motel shuttle service took me to the airport. I flew to Toronto, North Bay, and back to Timmins and home. Another mission accomplished.

August 13th., 1981. I obtained the necessary documents to Incorporate Harvest Field missionary work. Carl Haacke, Elmer Telford and I signed the papers and returned them to the lawyer.

September 4th., 1981 - A phone call from Great Whale River requested I come to baptize a number of Inuit believers before I leave for Florida. I drove to the Timmins airport. Flew in Austin's plane to Moosonee, Rupert's House, L.G.2 - the Hydro airport, then to Great Whale. Charlie and Eva Sappa met me at the airport and took me to their home. Inuit gathered for a good Bible Study especially on water baptism.

September 5th. - Great Whale River, Quebec, on the Hudson Bay. A few Inuit gathered here in this home, before I was able to get up. They asked more questions on water baptism. We had a precious time of Bible teaching. We discussed the questions of where we could hold a water baptismal service. We went out and walked to a number of sites. Another good Bible Study this evening till near 11 PM. It was decided we would have Great Whale River's first water baptismal service by immersion tomorrow.

September 6th. - Sunday, at Great Whale River. We all attended the morning service at the Anglican Church. Our water baptismal service was set for three o'clock. Many Inuit gathered in for a time of rejoicing and prayer. The Anglican minister came over and denounced this water baptismal service. He tried to persuade the candidates to back out. He accused me of being a trouble maker, and that I had more or less compelled these candidates to be baptized. But I explained to him that it was them who phoned me to come all the way up here, and they insisted on me to baptize them in water. We all walked down to the shore of the Great Whale River. I baptized seven of these wonderful Inuit Christians by immersion, to the glory of God. Had a good time of worship and Bible Study in the evening service.

September 7th. - At Great Whale River, Quebec, on the eastern shore of the Hudson Bay. Had another Bible Study and prayer meeting in the forenoon. Austin's plane arrived at 12. We flew to L.G.2, Rupert's House, Moosonee and to Timmins. Glad to be home again.

September 14th., 1981. Signed Harvest Field Society Incorporation papers at the lawyer's office.

October 4th., 1981 - A Finnish Christian man from Ramore, Ontario, and I, drove to Ottawa with the hopes to get the "Siberian 7" out of Russia. These seven were Christians who wanted to immigrate to the West. Russia refused. Now they were in the U.S.A. Embassy in Moscow.

October 5th. - We visited the Soviet Consulate. He was glad to see us and we had a friendly talk. Then we mentioned our purpose: to have the "Siberian 7" released in our care, and that we would pay all expenses involved, and that we already had two farms for the two families. But he said there was no chance at all of them being released. We even promised to go to Moscow and bring them to Canada, if we had the necessary papers for their release. But all our discussion was in vain. At least we tried our best, and I feel good about that.

October 6th. - Daniel, Tyyne and I started our trip south in our motorhome. Visited a few friends and spoke in a few meetings enroute

October 21st. - We crossed into Michigan. I shared in Many Full Gospel Business Men's Fellowship banquets as well as in church services.

October 30th. - Arrived in Cape Coral, Florida. 88 F.

February 5th., 1982. - Jim Waters, Owen Grant and I signed a Harvest Field charter for the United States, and opened an office in Jim and Betty Waters home. Jim Waters agreed to be our agent for the United States. We had many missionary meetings in many churches, some Baptist, Alliance, Assembly of God and Independents. I also shared in a few Full Gospel Business Men's Fellowship banquets. We thank the Lord for the number of souls saved and sick bodies healed.

April 2nd., 1982 - We left Cape Coral, Florida to begin our journey northward back to Canada.

April 29th. - We crossed the border at Windsor, Ontario, after having many meetings enroute. God touched many hearts and we thank the Lord for souls saved.

May 26th., 1982 - Arrived at our home in South Porcupine. God blessed in the many meetings along the way, too numerous to mention. We thank God for the many pastors and congregations who are interested enough in the Arctic missionary work to pray for and support it financially.

June 9th., 1982 - At South Porcupine. During my last visit to the Inuit believers at Payne Bay, Quebec, they had requested to have a church building. I had promised to send the materials by ship this summer. Today, Tyyne and I left home and drove south to Ottawa, then to Montreal.

June 10th. - We parked our motorhome at the Beaver Lumber building supply store. Roger, the owner of Beaver Lumber, and I worked on plans for the Payne Bay church.

June 10th. - 12th. - We made a list of all supplies needed, and started to build crates for the shipment.

June 14th. - 17th. In Montreal. Built many crates and packed insulation, shingles, tiles, oil stove, stove pipes, chimney, doors, windows, etc. Made up bundles of 2 X 4, 2 X 6, 2 X 8's. We loaded three trucks and delivered them to the harbour. Each crate and bundle had to be measured and weighed to arrive at the shipping cost. I paid the bill and Tyyne and I drove to Ottawa.

June 18th. - Arrived home in South Porcupine at 7:30 PM.

**2 Cor. 10:16 "To preach the gospel in
the regions beyond."**

June 30th. - Up at 4 AM. Drove out to Timmins airport at

5:30 AM. I flew in Austin's 748 plane to Kapuskasing, to Great Whale River - arrived at Cape Dorset on Baffin Island. God blessed in the service tonight and about a dozen came forward for prayer.

July 1st., 1982 - At Cape Dorset. The harbour here is full of ice. Inuit hunters travel by skidoo. A very good meeting in the church tonight. Many Inuit attended.

July 2nd. Three degrees C. Udjualuk arrived home from a hunting trip. He brought many ducks and duck eggs. We went to the First Air office and I purchased tickets for Udjualuk and I for a missionary trip north. Another good meeting tonight. Bible Study on Gal. 5.

July 3rd. - Visited a few homes in the forenoon. Quite a few Inuit came to visit me this afternoon, here in Udjualuk's home. These Inuit want a service each night while I am here. The subject in tonight's service was "Be Ready".

July 4th. - Sunday, Cape Dorset. A good crowd attended the morning service. My subject was "The Holy Spirit". Between 30 and 35 came forward for prayer. Many received the wonderful Baptism of the Holy Spirit. The church was packed full for the evening service. God gave me great liberty in preaching the Word. A good altar call followed when many came forward for prayer, salvation and healing.

July 5th. - Udjualuk and I flew to Frobisher Bay. I was asked to preach in the Pentecostal Church. 14 were in attendance; two of these came forward for prayer.

July 6th. - We flew to Resolute Bay, way above the Arctic Circle. We visited a few Inuit homes, as this was our first visit here. Met some nice families and we were able to share the gospel message. We stayed in one of the Inuit homes.

July 7th. - Visited a few more homes. Up against demoniac powers, had prayer and cast out demons in the name of Jesus. One nineteen year old Inuit girl accepted Jesus. It was cold and snowing all day.

July 8th. - At Resolute Bay. Distributed gospel literature in the English and Inuit languages. Shared the good news of salvation to a few interested persons.

July 9th. - We flew to Grise Fiord on Ellesmere Island. This is the last Inuit village nearest to the North Pole. This is our destination as the call of God on my life was "Go north and preach the gospel." So here we are - *"to the regions beyond."* I thank God for the privilege of taking the gospel to these Inuit people. And how God has provided for us - through our many friends, who have supported us in prayer and financially. I just feel great, knowing I have obeyed the call of God. But there is still much work to do, to win these Inuit to Jesus. Who suffered and died for each one.

July 10th. - Grise Fiord, N.W.T. The sun stays overhead night and day. It is as bright at midnight as it is at noon. These Inuit go to sleep when they get tired and sleepy. They eat when they are hungry.

I had very good talks to some Inuit who could understand and speak English. I had gospel literature and New Testaments, which I gave to them.

July 11th. - Sunday. Grise Fiord. I met the Anglican minister yesterday, and he asked me to preach in his church this morning. Udjualuk interpreted for me. The Word of God will not return void. The seed was sewn and I trust it fell upon good ground.

July 12th. - At Grise Fiord. Solid ice on the waters in front of the village. There are high mountains behind the village with great glaciers of ice moving constantly toward the ocean. I met some very nice people, who appeared somewhat interested in the gospel message. I gave out New Testaments. We trust that the Holy Spirit will work in their hearts and bring them to repentance and salvation in Jesus Christ.

July 13th. - Sun shines continuously, day and night. I have a room in the only "hotel". Five young men came to my room. I had talked to them the last few days as we met in the village. They said, "We have come to receive Jesus as our personal Saviour. Will you pray for us?" What a joy to lead these young men in the sinner's prayer of repentance and to invite Jesus into their hearts.

I took a walk just east of the village to take pictures of the large blocks of ice, as large as a house, pushed up by the ocean tide. Then I turned around and took pictures of the high mountain and beautiful glaciers behind me. I decided to walk back to the village, about one eighth of a mile away. When I reached the first houses, many Inuit came rushing out - hollering loudly and pointing past me. I looked over on my left, and saw two huge polar bears walking beside me. What a shock! I believe if I had started to run, they could have attacked and killed me. But with all this noise, they veered off toward the left and walked away.

One Inuit woman who could speak good English, said she had watched me taking the pictures, and she also saw those two polar bears stalking me, coming closer and closer. But when I would move, they would squat down, then crouching they came closer. Then I decided to walk back to the village. They were so close and yet I did not see them, till now. You see, these polar bears hunt people and kill them, but thank the Lord for His protecting care. Somebody must have been praying for me.

July 14th. - Wednesday. Both Udjualuk and I were asked to

preach in the weekly Anglican Church service. A good crowd attended, and a few came up for prayer. It seems that the gospel message is penetrating; and now we can witness some results. Praise the Lord!

It was in the summer of 1936, that the Lord called me to "Go north and preach the gospel". Now it is 1982, 46 years later, and that call has been fulfilled. All these many years, the Lord has used us to win hundreds of people to the Lord, and enabled us to build many churches for the whites, Indians and now for the Inuit.

July 15th. - At Grise Fiord, N.W.T. on Ellesmere Island. Up shortly after 6 AM. The plane arrived and we flew out to Resolute Bay - Nanisivik, and on to Pond Inlet. We stayed in Caleb Ootova's home. Had a good Bible Study this evening. Prayed for a number of people.

July 16th. - Pond Inlet. Witnessed to a few Inuit people. Another good evening service - this time in the Community Center, as the crowds were too great for a home meeting. God touched many hearts, as they came forward for prayer.

July 17th. - Caleb's wife had been away, with a hunting party of Inuit. She arrived home with a lot of narwhale hide and meat. What a feast - of raw whale meat - as the neighbours gathered in. But I wasn't hungry. Caleb's wife cooked some for me - which I ate. Another great service tonight - as God moved upon many hearts - more came forward and received Jesus as Saviour.

July 18th. - Sunday at Pond Inlet - on the north east coast of Baffin Island. We all attended the Anglican Church morning service. The Inuit insisted we have our own evening service. A good number attended - a few more saved and two received the Baptism of the Holy Spirit.

July 19th. - I purchased tickets for Udjualuk and I. $1,287.00 on my Visa card. A very good meeting this evening - in another home. Many Inuits left the village this morning to go camping, hunting and fishing.

July 20th. - Pond Inlet. Udjualuk and I flew on the First Air plane to Igloolik. A meeting was requested and a good number of people gathered. God blessed and gave great liberty to preach the Word. I told the people about receiving a letter from a lady here to whom I gave my card which had the calendar and scriptures on it. She wrote and said, "since I've read these Bible verses I have accepted Jesus as my Saviour". I asked whether she was in the service and someone spoke up and said: "she is your interpreter". When I gave the altar call, many came forward for prayer, some for salvation, others for healing and others to be better Christians.

July 21st. - At Igloolik, N.W.T. It's very cold and foggy. I went to the Hudson Bay Co. store and bought a little over $50.00 of groceries, which I carried in a couple of hand bags. Another great meeting tonight and a good altar call.

July 22 - Igloolik. Had good opportunity to share with some today. Praise the Lord for a very good evening service. Many came forward for prayer.

July 23rd. - Igloolik, N.W.T. Went out visiting this forenoon. A white lady, I believe she is a nurse, came to visit the home where I am staying. She was interested in the gospel message and asked many questions. She accepted Jesus. Many of the men, Christian and non-Christian have gone camping, hunting or fishing for this week end. We still have enough people for an evening service - which God honoured with His Presence.

July 24th. - Igloolik. Had a good visit in Sandra's home, the lady who accepted Jesus yesterday. A very interesting Bible Study, prayer meeting tonight.

July 25th. - Sunday. The strong wind has blown very much loose ice into the bay in front of the village. We had morning and evening services in which I preached from the Word. Also listened to many wonderful testimonies of God's saving grace and His protection in times of danger.

July 26th. - At Igloolik. A Twin Otter plane arrived and Udjualuk and I flew to Nanisivik where a big lead mine is operating. It's cold - minus two degrees with a strong wind. We stayed in Sam and Louise Kangoks home. Held a very good meeting and two Inuit women accepted Jesus.

July 27th. - At Nanisivik, N.W.T., 450 miles north of the Arctic Circle. The mining company has a community church here. We held our evening service here and a good crowd gathered in. I preached in English and Udjualuk preached in Inuit. A good time of prayer followed.

July 28th. - At Nanisivik. We planned to go to Arctic Bay today, but Udjualuk took sick after service last night and could not sleep at all. The people at Arctic Bay, which is about 18 miles from here, were expecting a service, so I took a taxi there. The house was packed full of people. I counted at least 60 from where I was standing. Our leader at Arctic Bay is Charlie, but he is away narwhale hunting. God blessed in tonight's service, and twelve came forward for salvation. I believe it was after midnight when Charlie returned with Arctic Char, seal, and four Narwhale with their ivory tusks.

July 29th. - In Charlie Inuaraks' home. Another service held all forenoon. We dedicated three Inuit babies. I had to rush to Nanisivik airport, where Udjualuk was waiting for me. Nordair 737 jet arrived. We flew to Frobisher Bay and I continued on to Montreal. Udjualuk will fly to Cape Dorset tomorrow. I have a room at the International Hotel for $37.00.

July 30th. - In Montreal. I flew Air Canada jet to Toronto, changed planes for Timmins. Carl Haacke met me and drove me home - sweet home, tired but rejoicing.

August 11th., 1982 - The Laotian boat people have finished their studies in English, and asked me to help find jobs for them. We contacted many companies but did not find any openings.

August 12th. - I got up at 4.45 AM. Drove to the Timmins Airport. Boarded Austin's 748 turbo jet. Flew to Great Whale River. Got David Sappa and we flew to Sanikuluaq - which is on the Belcher Island, N.W.T.

August 13th. - at Sanikuluaq on Belcher Island. We stayed in the only place for transients to stay, at $90.00 each per night. We were able to witness to some of the Inuit, but decided to fly back to Great Whale, as a plane was coming this afternoon.

Our Christians requested a Bible Study in Joses' home. We had a wonderful time around the Word. This meeting lasted till two AM.

August 14th. - Great Whale River, Quebec, on the Hudson Bay. We visited a few homes. Elizabeth, one of our Inuit Christian women, requested to hold our evening service in her home. A good crowd gathered, as we taught from the Word.

August 15th. - Sunday. Great Whale River. We attended the morning service at the Anglican Church. Had a good Bible Study this afternoon and another one this evening till 11:45 PM. Many questions were asked about problems, and were answered from the Bible.

August 16th. - Three of the Inuit young men, 20, 24 and 27 years old, requested water baptism - so we gathered at a small lake north east of the village and had a wonderful time of rejoicing. A very good Bible Study tonight till about 11 PM. Good crowd.

August 17th. - Plane arrived and I flew south to Fort George, Paint Hills, Eastmain, Rupert's House, Moosonee, Timmins - and home again.

August 25th. - The one Laotian woman and her brother received a letter from Thailand from another brother, who with his wife and five children, asked for help to get them to Canada. We gathered at Carl Haacke's home for a Boat People meeting. We agreed to bring them over. We all donated a total of $2,700.00 to start the fund.

August 26th. - South Porcupine. I visited the Immigration office in Timmins and started procedure for our second group of Boat people.

August 30th. - A phone call from the Insurance Company in Montreal, that the ship carrying our church building supplies to Payne Bay had caught fire - which was put out; but a lot of damage was done to the cargo.

September 1st to 13th., 1982 - I worked in the office. Took the Laotian men for job applications. Word from the shipping company in Montreal is that our supplies on ship were not damaged. The ship proceeded to Payne Bay.

September 14th. - South Porcupine - five degrees C. Packed things in our motor home and started our journey south.

September 16th. - We crossed the border into the United States.

September 21st. Arrived at Cape Coral, Florida.

September 29th. - My wife Tyyne and I left Cape Coral, drove to Christian Retreat at Bradenton - van to Tampa Airport. We flew to New York City - boarded TWA flight to Israel.

September 30th. - to October 12th. - We landed in England - then flew on to Israel. Had a wonderful time, visiting many places mentioned in the Bible. A very large crowd gathered in the "All Nation Auditorium". Prime Minister Begin came and spoke to us. We took part in the Feast of Tabernacles. Arrived back at Christian Retreat tired, but rejoicing in the Lord.

October 13th. to December 16th., 1982 More than enough office work, plus preaching at various churches and sharing at Full Gospel Business Men's Banquets.

December 17th - Cape Coral, Florida. A lawyer phoned from Timmins that I must fly up to settle an estate. I got up at 5 AM. Brother Eugene Yakas drove me to Fort Myers jet port. I flew to Toronto, changed planes and flew to Timmins. Twenty below zero and plenty of snow on the ground.

December 18th. to 21st. - Worked with the lawyer on Mrs. Wraight's estate. Received $14,153.54 for Harvest Field missionary work in the Canadian Arctic.

December 22nd. - South Porcupine, 26 below zero. I flew to North Bay, Toronto, changed planes and flew to Tampa, Florida and then on to Fort Myers. Eugene Yakas met me and we drove to Cape Coral and home.

Chapter 8

His Continuing Goodness

**Psalm 65:11 "Thou crownest the year with Thy
goodness; and thy paths drop fatness.**

January 15th. - 1983. Cape Coral, Florida. Celebrated our
45th. wedding anniversary at Morrison's Restaurant - with a
group of friends.

January 17th. Cape Coral, Florida. Don and Jean Shire from
Bobcaygeon, Ontario came to see us about missionary work in
the Canadian Arctic. Don is a good pilot; and asked if he could
use our Harvest Field plane in the Arctic for missionary work
as he is well able to pay the insurance, all operating costs and
all expenses. We agreed to let him have the plane, since it
would not cost Harvest Field anything, and since the plane
was just sitting idle at Steinbach, Manitoba. I telephoned Ike
Innes in Steinback about Don flying our plane.

January 18th. to March 23rd. - Cape Coral, Florida. We've
travelled in our motor home to preach in various churches,
mostly on the east side of Florida. Also printed and mailed our
Harvest Field news letters each month - usually around 450
copies. March 23rd. - I have extreme pains around my stomach and sides. Dr. Dawson checked me and said, "You have
shingles." These may last, he said, for six weeks - and that I
must take pain pills every four hours and rest a lot.

March 31st., 1983 - Cape Coral, Florida. We loaded our
motor home and began our trip north, back to Canada, although the doctor advised us not to travel. We prayed for
healing and the pain subsided somewhat.

April 1st to 18th., 1983 - Travelling north - speaking in meetings in various churches. Crossed Ontario border on April
18th. Cold and snowing.

April 19th. - Five degrees below zero C. to five degrees
above zero C.

April 20th. to May 16th. - Held many meetings enroute. We
thank the Lord for the many open doors, and the many souls
saved along the way. Also for the prayers and financial support of God's people.

We arrived home in South Porcupine on May 16th. at 7:30
PM.

May 24th., 1983 - Don and Jean Shire flew into Timmins airport from Steinbach, Manitoba - with our Harvest Field missionary plane, 185 Cessna, C-GVXV. Then they flew north.

June 1st., 1983 - Up at 3 AM. Drove to Timmins airport. In Austin Airways 748 Turbo jet, we took off at 4:30 AM, flew to Great Whale River and on to Cape Dorset. A large crowd attended our evening service, and many Inuit crowded the altar for prayer. We thank God for the hunger for more of God, in the hearts of these Inuit people.

June 2nd. - Udjualuk and another Inuit went hunting for caribou. They shot two. Now we have plenty of meat to eat. Another great service tonight. Minnie, Udjualuk's wife, led the singing and I preached to a large crowd. Many responded to the altar call.

June 3rd. - I purchased two plane tickets for Udjualuk and I - $1,358.00. Visited two houses. Prepared for service. The church was packed with people. Minnie again led in the singing and I preached. God blessed and touched many hearts as they came forward for prayer.

June 4th. - Four degrees C. below zero. Had a good Bible Study this morning. Udjualuk and I flew to Frobisher Bay on Baffin Island, N.W.T. We visited a few houses, and Udjualuk preached in our evening service in Mosesee Kowirk's home.

June 5th. - Folks here slept late as they don't have to work. Attended church service this morning and we had caribou for dinner, then I visited another family. At 6 PM we returned home after a visit to the hospital and a number of other homes. Udjualuk spoke at the Inuit service tonight and then several Inuit came home for a feast of raw, frozen caribou hind quarter. I had a cup of tea and some bannock.

June 6th. - Very cool. Visited some sick folk and prayed for them. A very good Bible Study, and good attendance.

June 7th. - Frobisher Bay on Baffin Island, N.W.T. While out visiting, I stopped at a roadside stand and purchased a cup of coffee and a hamburger which cost $6.00. Another great Bible Study in Mosesee's house. A precious time of sincere prayer followed.

June 8th. - Igloolik. There was ice as far as I could see. At Hall's Beach while waiting for our flight, two Inuit men were leaving for Igloolik by skidoo for it's like winter with so much snow and ice. Left at 7:10 PM and one hour later was in the service at Igloolik. A number gave testimony before I preached.

June 9th. - Minus 4 degrees. Got groceries this morning and the service lasted from 7 PM to 9:20. Many souls were touched as they came for prayer. Then we had a business meeting and following it, I had fellowship with a Christian government man who was waiting for me. In the business meeting, the 8 Inuit men who have good salaries felt they could build their church when the time comes. They still have a little room in their present building, but at times, it's packed out. Their decision will release us to help elsewhere where the need is greater.

June 10th. - While walking down the street I met a fine man I presume is in his 30's. I began to witness to him but he said "I'm born again. Last year was the very worst: drinking and fighting. My wife and children would have to stay in a neighbour's house. But now we have a lovely home." He is manager of the Co-op Restaurant and Coffee Bar. He invited me in for a hamburger and coffee. There was a good response to the service tonight and one lady whom they had prayed for a long time, came to the altar and accepted Jesus. Udjualuk also preached. Also, after the service, a young man came to the house and accepted Jesus.

June 11th. - I flew First Air to Hall's Beach, changed to Nordair 737 jet: flew to Frobisher Bay, Fort Chimo and on to Montreal.

June 12th and 13th. - In Montreal. I rented a Budget car to purchase supplies for the Cape Dorset Full Gospel Church. I finished in time to fly Air Canada to Toronto, then to Timmins and home.

June 27th. - I received a phone call from Great Whale River, Quebec, on the Hudson Bay east coast. Our Christians there needed a church building as our membership has outgrown house meetings. So today I flew to Great Whale River. Had a good Bible Study in Charles and Eva Sappa's home.

June 28th. to July 1st., 1983 - Had many discussions about a church building. I talked to the mayor, who told me that a brand new village for the Inuit people is being built about 85 miles further north, along the Hudson Bay coast; and that when it is completed, most of the Inuits will be moving up there. We held good Bible Studies for the three days and nights I stayed in Great Whale River. Souls were saved and the Christians edified. I flew home to Timmins airport and drove my car to South Porcupine.

July 8th. to 11th. - I received a phone call from Pastor Michael Sheeshee at Attawapiskat, Ontario on James Bay asking me to come up. I flew up on Austin's 748 from Timmins. Had good Bible Studies during the day and evangelistic services in the evenings for three days. A few Indians were saved and the Christians encouraged in the Lord. I returned home by Austin's plane. Our Harvest Field plane piloted by Don Shire was up on Baffin Island in missionary work.

July 12th. to August 1st., 1983 Made many applications for jobs for the Laotian Boat people. Travelled all around Timmins, Schumacher and South Porcupine for days looking for work. Also we needed another apartment or house for the new family of seven Laotian Boat people which should arrive soon from Thailand. On August 1st. we held a Boat people meeting and decided to purchase an apartment house with four apartments, two to be used for our boat people and the other two to be rented out. We purchased Ed Harjula's apartment house at 122 Fourth Avenue in Schumacher. We had to notify the tenants in two apartments that we needed the apartments.

August 2nd. to 10th. Carl Haacke and I gathered up furniture and bedding supplies for the new Laotian family. In the meantime we rented a temporary home, till our apartment was vacated. At 4:30 PM. August 10th., a group of us met our Laotian family at the airport. The newspaper reporters and camera man took pictures and also the television news crew was on hand. A good publicity story in the media was presented.

August 12th. - I performed the wedding for two of our first group of Laotian Boat people - Bounlert Phomsouvanh and Khantank Bounprasueth - in the South Porcupine Pentecostal Church. It was the bride's brother and his wife and family who had just arrived from the refugee camp in Thailand. The father, Oudome Bounprasueth was a pilot in the Vietnam war. His plane was shot down by the communist and Oudome was captured and placed in a terrible prison with hundreds of other men. One by one these prisoners were dying for lack of medical aid. Oudome thought of some way to escape - before he too would die. One night he managed to escape and swam the Mekong River to Thailand. Many weeks later his wife and family were able to come to the same refugee camp. Now, just two days after his arrival in Timmins, he said, "I want to go to work".

August 13th. to September 9th. - In the meantime, the other three Laotian men found jobs - through the many applications we made. And now, since August 13th. - we've looked for a job for Oudome. Today, September 9th., Oudome began to work at La Fleur's Gardens. Lafleur has many greenhouses and grows millions of spruce seedlings for the government. Oudome had never worked in a nursery but he was willing to learn and he did so very quickly.

September 13th., 1983 South Porcupine. Zero degrees temperature - ice on the water puddles. Winter is coming.

September 14th. to 29th. - Office work; also a lot of work to help get the Laotian people in their new apartments. At last they are settled.

September 30th. to October 18th. Packed supplies in our motor home and started our trip south to Montreal. Had very good meetings enroute. I showed pictures of the work in the Arctic.

October 19th., 1983 - Montreal. For the past many months, a few of my friends mentioned they would be pleased to form a group for a trip to Israel. Sarah Cookie, an Inuit from Great Whale River, Dawn Adams, my niece, and I flew to New York. Here we changed planes and began our flight to Israel with the rest of our group, who gathered at Kennedy Airport.

October 20th. - On a Royal Jordanian 747 plane. We landed and refuelled at Vienna, Austria and flew on to Amman, Jordan, where we stayed for the night.

October 21st. to 26th. - Had a wonderful time in Israel. We crossed over from Jordan to Israel at the Allenby Bridge. We visited Jericho, Masada, Joppa, Nazareth, Tiberias, had a boat trip on the Sea of Galilee to Capernaum, and Bethlehem.

On October 24th., the huge bomb blew up part of the U.S. building in Beirut, Lebanon killing more than 200 U.S. soldiers. In Jerusalem, we visited the Upper Room, Gethsemane, the Wailing Wall, the Garden Tomb, etc., etc.

On October 26th., we returned to Amman Jordan and flew back to the States with our Canadian group continuing on to Montreal.

October 30th. - We arrived in Cape Coral, Florida in our motor home.

October 31st. to January 26th., 1984. Our stay in warm, sunny Florida was filled with office work, answering letters and printing our Harvest Field newsletter. Daniel and I helped build a church in Sebring for two weeks. We had meetings and showed Arctic slides. We thank the Lord for souls saved, *who passed from death unto life, from the broad way which leads to hell - to the narrow way which leads to Heaven.*

January 27th. - A few of us from Christian Retreat at Bradenton, Florida, flew south to Haiti. We landed at Port-au-Prince, and booked into the Caribbean Christian Center.

January 28th. - Attended the Gospel Crusade Convention for ministers of Haiti. I shared with the ministers of what God is doing in the Canadian Arctic.

January 29th. - In Haiti, at the Gospel Crusade Convention I was asked to share further on the Canadian Arctic missionary work. We travelled to one of the Haitian churches for the evening service where I preached the Word. When I gave the altar call, six came forward for salvation, and many others for healing. God was in that place, and miracles were done in the name of Jesus.

January 30th. - We drove north in Haiti, and up in the hills we visited a church which also had a day school for 161 students. We were able to share the gospel and encourage the students to *"Seek ye first the Kingdom of God, and His righteousness."*

January 31st. We drove south west and visited other Gospel Crusade churches, schools and an orphanage. Haiti is one of the poorest nations in the Western World. High School teacher's salary is $60.00 per month. Public School teacher's salary is $30.00 per month - if the money is available.

We met and talked with two teachers who were faithfully teaching the students, in spite of the fact, they had not received any salary during the last year of 1983. When Gerald Derstine, founder of Gospel Crusade in Bradenton, Florida, told our group of the situation, we took an offering right there on the bus; enough for the two teachers for the 1983 year. Praise the Lord! Great rejoicing and appreciation were verbalized by these two teachers.

February 1st., 1984 - We flew back to the States. Drove to Christian Retreat at Bradenton. Then we drove to Cape Coral, Florida. It was a wonderful experience.

February 2nd. to April 1st. - We were kept busy in Florida. Had good opportunities to share and show my Arctic slides in different churches and groups. Also had a one hour of sharing in the Florida University at Fort Myers, Florida.

April 2nd., 1984 - Left Cape Coral, Florida in our motor home and started our trip north.

April 5th. - Crossed the Ontario border at Windsor at 6:15 PM.

April 7th. to May 2nd., 1984 - We recrossed the border into the States. Had numerous meetings in many different churches and also was on TV programs. We thank God for these open doors to the Harvest Field missionary work, and also for the souls saved in these meetings.

May 3rd., 1984 - We crossed into Ontario at the Ivy Lee Bridge just north east of Kingston, Ontario. We drove through to Montreal.

May 4th. - I flew from Montreal Dorval Airport to Great Whale River, Quebec on the Hudson Bay. Our Inuit Christians here, had asked me to come up to see about building a church. We had a very good Bible Study tonight. A good crowd had gathered and the meeting ended at 11:45 PM. God blessed. A few came forward to accept Jesus. Others asked for healing.

May 5th. - A good number of Christian Inuit men gathered to discuss the building of a church here.

The government had promised a site for our church at the new village of Umiujaq about 85 miles north of here, on the Hudson Bay coast - but said it may take three or four years or longer before matters would be finalized. So our men here at Great Whale River - decided to build a church here to worship in. We decided on the size of the building and started to make a list of the needed building supplies. Another good meeting tonight - the largest crowd yet - till 11 PM.

May 6th. - Sunday at Great Whale River. The people requested a communion service, so we gathered in Willie Kumarluk's house and had a precious time around the communion table. People wept as they were reminded of the suffering Jesus went through - then He gave His life - for our salvation.

Louis Gunn requested that the evening service be held in his home. The largest crowd yet gathered in. My message was on the theme of "The soon coming of Jesus". Many came forward for prayer.

On my last visit to Great Whale River, Louis Gunn had come to visit me, in another house where I was staying. He was not saved, but I soon found out, that is why he came. He wanted to receive Jesus as his Saviour; which he did. Praise the Lord!

May 7th. - Last night the Christians here at Great Whale River, took an offering to help pay for the church building supplies. The offering totalled $4,500.00. I flew back to Montreal where Tyyne and Dan were waiting in our motor home for me. We drove north of Montreal to the lumber supply company where I always buy our supplies.

May 8th. - Roger, the owner of the lumber company, started to work at 6:30 AM - checking over the list of supplies needed for the Great Whale River church building

May 9th. - Montreal. I paid $19,000.00 deposit on these supplies. We drove to the harbour, and arranged for shipping to Great Whale River. We shared in the Finnish Pentecostal meeting tonight.

May 10th. - Up at 3 AM. Started to drive at 3:45 AM to Ottawa, then to Bancroft to visit my sister Cora Gaebel.

May 11th. - Up at 4:45 AM. Drove to my other sister's home, Mrs. Frank Dewey at Gooderham. Drove north to Huntsville, North Bay - to Kirkland Lake. Visited our second daughter Grace and her husband, Glen Adams, pastors of the Pentecostal Church here.

May 12th. - Glen and Grace decided to purchase the house they were living in, and asked if we could help them with a loan, which we did. Attended a Full Gospel Business Men's Banquet and many went forward for prayer.

May 12th. - At Kirkland Lake. We drove to South Porcupine amidst snow flurries, and moved into our house, as the winter tenants had just moved out.

May 20th. - Don and Jean Shire had returned from the Arctic with our missionary plane, which was now at Orillia Airways. Our son, Dan, and I drove from South Porcupine to Orillia.

May 21st. - We loaded the plane skiis and cargo pod into the car, and Dan left to drive back home. I flew the plane, which was on wheels to the Timmins Airport. Carl Haacke met me and drove me home in his car.

June 1st.. 1984 - Marvin Jones, pastor of Faith Chapel in North Bay - had spoken to me about purchasing our plane. So today, he phoned to fly the plane to North Bay on Monday.

June 4th. - Monday. I flew our Harvest Field Missionary plane 185 Cessna, CGVXV to North Bay.

Marvin Jones purchased our plane for missionary work among the Indians in northern Ontario.

June 7th. - South Porcupine, Ontario. Phone calls from the Arctic requested me to come for meetings. Tyyne and Dan drove me to Timmins airport. I flew to Toronto, and then to Montreal. Stayed at the Airport Inn there for $37.00.

June 8th. - Montreal: flew in Nordair 737 jet to Fort Chimo. My Inuit brother George Koneak met me at the airport and took me to his house. We had a good evening of fellowship and sharing.

June 9th. - Fort Chimo, Quebec. Weather not good for flying. George Koneak and I visited a few homes and at the hospital.

June 10th. - Sunday. Snowing and blowing. We attended the morning service at the Anglican Church. One Christian French couple invited us to have a service in their home this evening. A few others gathered in. I shared the Word with them. They were encouraged in the Lord.

June 11th. - Word came to me that a plane was flying to Wakeham Bay, but it was full. George Koneak drove me to the airport - where Johnny May had his private commercial plane service. They were just warming up the engine when we arrived. One seat was empty, so I had a free flight to Wakeham Bay on this charter.

June 12th. - Wakeham Bay, Quebec on the shores of Hudson Strait, where we built the church in 1979. Snow flurries and freezing weather. A good service - held in the church - also prayer time.

June 13th. - Air Inuit's twin Otter came in. I flew on to Sugluk, then to Quaqtaq. The weather is very poor for flying. A fair crowd gathered in the church, built here in 1980. These Inuit Christians really love to worship and praise the Lord. We had a good altar service after the Bible Study.

June 14th. - Cold north wind. Had good visits with Matthew, Johnnie and Bob Deer this afternoon. Some new men and women attended our evening service as I ministered the Word. A prayer time followed.

June 15th. - At Quaqtak. Prayed for a sick seven year old Inuit boy. He accepted Jesus as Saviour and Healer. I flew into Payne Bay where our Full Gospel church was built in 1982.

Many Inuits gathered in church for our evening service. God blessed and one fine young Inuit woman accepted Jesus as Saviour. Had a precious time of prayer.

June 16th. - Payne Bay. Bible Study in the forenoon and afternoon, followed by a great meeting in the church tonight. God blessed and touched many hearts.

June 17th. - Sunday. A precious time of praise and worship in this morning's service. A very large crowd gathered for the evening service. Three came forward for salvation. At 10 PM we held a water baptismal service. What a great time we had!

June 18th. - Payne Bay, northern Quebec. Visited a few sick folk and prayed for them. Air Inuit plane arrived. I flew to Fort Chimo, then by Nordair jet 737 to Montreal.

June 19th. - Rented a car, to look after some business.

June 20th. - Flew to Toronto, Timmins and home.

July 12th., 1984 - An Inuit Conference was planned for the Arctic, to be held at Cape Dorset, N.W.T. on Baffin Island. I invited Brother Graydon Meek and Brother Tom Easton to come as speakers. I flew to Toronto and on to Montreal.

July 13th. - Brothers Meek and Easton arrived and we flew north to Fort Chimo, to Frobisher Bay and on to Cape Dorset. A great crowd filled the church as I ministered the Word, followed by a precious time of prayer.

July 14th. to July 20th. - At Cape Dorset, Inuit Full Gospel Bible Conference. Many Inuit leaders had arrived and three great meetings were held each day. Brother Graydon Meek, Brother Tom Easton and I alternated in teaching and preaching.

A wonderful spirit of praise and worship prevailed the total conference. Many testified how much they appreciated a conference like this. Pastors and church workers had come from the Ungava Bay area of northern Quebec, also the settlements along the Hudson Strait, and way down the coast of Hudson Bay. Also, representatives had come from Igloolik, Arctic Bay, Nanisivik, Pond Inlet and Frobisher Bay. A great water baptismal service was held inside the church as the local men had built a tank for this purpose. It was a time of rejoicing as a good number of new converts took their stand for the Lord and were baptized.

Another great service was the communion service, as we partook of the bread and grape juice, a symbol of Jesus' broken body and shed blood. It was a time we will not soon forget, as many worshipped the Lord with tears streaming down their faces. We decided to hold our next Bible conference at Arctic Bay, North West Territories.

July 21st. - Brother Graydon Meek, Brother Tom Easton and I flew back to Frobisher Bay, Fort Chimo and Montreal.

July 22nd. - We flew to Toronto. Brothers Meek and Easton drove to Hamilton and I flew to Timmins and home.

July 26th. - The Laotian Boat people rented a hall and put on a delicious Laotian Canadian food party for all those who had a part in sponsoring them to come to Canada from Thailand. A good number of people attended and we had a wonderful time of fellowship and eating.

August 17th., 1984 - A phone call from Cape Dorset informed me of a serious problem in the church. They asked me to come up to settle it. So today I flew from Timmins to Montreal.

August 18th. - I flew north to Frobisher Bay by Nordair jet 737, and by First Air 748 to Cape Dorset. I held quite a few meetings with the parties involved with much prayer and waiting on God for wisdom.

August 19th. - Sunday at Cape Dorset. A decision was reached and victory proclaimed. Two great services today as the people rejoiced at the decision made. In both morning and evening services as I shared from the Word, God gave great liberty and the crowds which filled the church rejoiced.

August 20th. and 21st. - Great interest was shown as we had Bible teachings each day, followed by earnest prayer meetings.

August 22nd. - I flew back to Frobisher Bay and on to Montreal.

August 23rd. - I flew on to Toronto, North Bay, Timmins and home.

September 2nd to 5th., 1984 - I was named as an executor of Horley's will. So Tyyne and I loaded our things in our motor home and drove south to Tehkummah on Manitoulin Island. We announced a sale of all household furniture and farming equipment. Special items were given to certain people named in the will. We divided the farm into two parcels. One parcel included the house and barn while the other was for pasture. Named in the will were relatives who received what was designated in the will. We had a lawyer to assist us. Most of the estate was settled, except for a land sale, which was advertised in the Toronto paper. This was sold and settled later. A good portion of the proceeds were given to the "Shantyman Association" and to "Harvest Field" missionary work.

September 17th. -Packed things in the motor home, and started our trip south. Had meetings in North Bay, Burks Falls, Haliburton, Bancroft, Apsley, Deseronto, Odessa and Napanee. We crossed the U.S. border at the Ivy Lee Bridge at 9 AM on October first.

November 29th., 1984 - I received a call from Kirkland Lake to come and be the speaker at the church we pastored in

1936. Tyyne and I flew north from Fort Myers jet port to Atlanta, Pittsburgh, Toronto and up to Timmins. Our daughter Grace and son Dan met us and drove us to Kirkland Lake. Very good communion service in their lovely new church on December first and second.

December 3rd., 1984 - Tyyne and I flew south to Fort Myers in Florida

December 19th. - Tyyne had a gall stone operation in Lee Memorial hospital in Fort Myers.

March 3rd., 1985. Cape Coral, Florida. All arrangements had been made for our Inuit Bible Conference at Arctic Bay, N.W.T. on the north west coast of Baffin Island. I flew from Tampa, Florida to Pittsburgh and Cleveland and on to Montreal.

March 4th. - Flew in Nordair's 737 jet to Frobisher Bay and on to Nanisivik - 45 degrees below zero. A van took us to Arctic Bay. Many of our Full Gospel Fellowship pastors and church workers boarded the plane at Frobisher Bay and we flew to Nanisivik. Wonderful service with a good altar call of dedication, then I called for any unsaved. One fine, well dressed Eskimo lady came forth and accepted Jesus.

March 5th. to 13th. 48 degrees below zero. Our Bible Conference started with a good prayer meeting here in the church where Charlie Inuarak is pastor. We invited Graydon Meek and Wayne Moore to assist in teaching. A wonderful spirit of love prevailed. Our morning session started at nine o'clock, a coffee break at 10:30 and the second morning session at 10:45 to 12 noon. Also, two sessions each afternoon with a great public meeting each night. Quite a number accepted Jesus in the evening services. We held a water baptismal service for twelve candidates. Also a precious time at the communion service.

The weather was very cold. One morning when I went to open the church for prayer, I found the oil frozen in the line and the oil fire out. The church was very cold. We all packed into pastor Charlie's home for the 8 AM prayer meeting, while two men worked on the stove and got it thawed out. Each evening the church was packed full with many standing on all sides, at the back, and also up front around the platform. We thank God for a great outpouring of His Holy Spirit, and the great work of grace upon so many who attended.

March 14th. - A terrific snow blizzard, with very low temperatures below zero - plus the wind chill factor, making temperatures 65 to 70 degrees below zero. We held morning sessions, then had to pack quickly and drive to Nanisivik airport. We flew back to Montreal, praising the Lord for all His many blessings.

March 15th. - I left Montreal at 9:30 AM and flew back to

Tampa, Florida. Archie and Jean McLean met me and we drove to Christian Retreat at Bradenton. I then drove to Cape Coral.

April 8th., 1985 - Left Cape Coral, Florida with our motor home and began our trip north. Had a few meetings enroute and showed Arctic slides.

April 17th. - We crossed the border at Windsor. Had good missionary meetings in Chatham, Oil Springs, two different churches in Sarnia, Komoka, Grassie, Toronto, Apsley and arrived home in South Porcupine on May 2nd.

May 15th., 1985 - I had a phone call from Great Whale River about a problem. It seems that two Inuit women from another village had come and told our congregation, that if a couple were married before being saved, they could separate and marry someone else. I had to phone Jim and Lena White of Sarnia to ask them to accompany me to Great Whale River. I flew to Toronto from Timmins where I met the Whites, and then we flew to Montreal.

May 16th. - In Montreal. We flew north to Great Whale River. Willie Kumarluk, our church secretary, opened his home for us to stay. A good crowd gathered in Charlie and Eva Sappa's home for an evening service. God blessed an a good prayer meeting followed.

May 17th. - I visited a few Christian homes. Some of our Inuit men and I checked for a site to build our church when the materials would arrive this summer. Jim White preached a good message in the evening service which was followed by a good altar service.

May 18th. - Great Whale River. Quite a few Christians came over, to where we were staying. We had a good Bible Study and time of prayer this morning. Udjualuk Etidloie arrived and he preached a good message on "the love of God" in the evening service.

May 19th. - Sunday. We all fasted till 2:30 PM. I preached in the morning service in Charlie and Eva's home. Had a big Canada Goose for dinner. Brother Jim White preached in the evening service. We met some who were causing dissension and tried to talk with them, but they insisted they were right. So we had to announce that they were no longer associated with our church.

May 20th. - Great Whale River. Visited a few families. A white man accepted Jesus as Saviour this afternoon. Tonight was the best service yet. A good crowd attended and one Inuit man was saved.

May 21st. - Visited a few homes. Then I packed up and flew to Montreal, Toronto and Timmins, and back home again.

June 3rd. to 5th., 1985 I am in Montreal to order all the supplies for the church building at Great Whale River. I helped to build crates and packed insulation and smaller articles inside. We also made up bundles of plywood, studding, floor joists, rafters, etc. I left Montreal this evening.

June 25th. The big day for our granddaughter Sandra was getting married so Tyyne and I flew to Fort Myers, Florida.

June 27th. - Wedding rehearsal at the First Assembly of God in Fort Myers.

June 29th. - I assisted Pastor Deaton of First Assembly, in the wedding of Frank Grauer and our granddaughter Sandra. A very large reception was held at the Country Club Inn. Our second daughter Grace Adams, Tyyne and I flew back to Canada, July second.

July 6th to 7th., 1985 I was requested to be speaker at special services at Faith Chapel, Attawapiskat, Ontario on James Bay. I flew up on the sixth. A great crowd gathered for the evening service. Sunday, July 7th. was a great day for the congregation here. God blessed in both the morning and evening services. Many responded to the altar call and came up for salvation, healing and the Baptism of the Holy Spirit. Gregg Sheeshish, the pastor, was greatly encouraged to see the wonderful move of the Holy Spirit upon these Indian people.

July 8th. - I flew south to Moosonee, Timmins and back home to South Porcupine.

July 22nd. - Received a phone call from Great Whale River, that the ship with our church building supplies had arrived from Montreal. I left Timmins in Austin's 748 Turbo jet and flew north. Stopped at all the villages along the James Bay coast up in to Hudson Bay and then to Great Whale River. A good meeting was held tonight at Sappa's home.

July 23rd. to 24th. - At Great Whale River. We held many business meetings about the new church building. Our Inuit people were told that the new village of Umiujaq would soon be completed, and they would move there. So why build the church at Great Whale River?

I met the man in charge of the new village. He promised to exchange our building supplies, for a good mobile unit already at Umiujaq. I took this proposition before the people here, and they agreed to accept. We signed this agreement with the authorities of Umiujaq. All were satisfied.

July 25th. to 26th. - I flew north to Povungnituk. Our Inuit Christians gathered in a home, and we had a great meeting together till 11:30 PM. A good time of prayer followed. Meetings were held both evenings.

July 27th. - At Povungnituk. I flew north to Ivugivik on the point where the Hudson Strait and Hudson Bay meets. Quite a few people have been saved here since my first visit. Now the main families requested a church building, as they have been meeting in homes.

A big crowd packed Lucassie's home for the evening service which lasted till 11 PM. The power of God descended, and miracles of salvation and healing took place.

July 28th. - Sunday. I preached in both the morning and evening services. While the morning service was on, word was brought to the parents of the home where the service was, that their little baby had died. But they know they shall see him again and even now the little one is with Jesus, laughing and playing. Today six young men and women accepted Jesus as Saviour.

July 29th. - At Ivugivik, Quebec. The men here insisted strongly that supplies be shipped in this summer. But the supply ship from Montreal was now here and unloading. I met with the Captain and asked if he would be bringing another ship load to Ivugivik this summer. He said "Yes", and he must hurry back to Montreal, get loaded and back here before the freeze up, but he didn't know if there would be room for our church building material. He said: "Phone Montreal and they will let you know."

I phoned Montreal and explained the situation, that a church building was needed here and asked if there would be any room for the supplies on the ship. "Yes," he replied, "We've done business with you before, and we will have room in the ship for your supplies." "But," he continued, "come quickly to Montreal and get all your material ready; crated and bundled, and bring them to the harbour as soon as possible."

July 30th. - I was able to get a seat on the Air Inuit plane and I flew to Great Whale River. Another good service tonight in Josie's home.

July 31st. All seats on Nordair's 737 jet were taken. I was advised to "stand by". Praise the Lord! I was motioned to go ahead and board the plane, and we flew south.

August 3rd., 1985 - At South Porcupine, Ontario. We packed things in our motor home and started on our trip to Montreal. Got as far as New Liskeard and stopped for the night.

August 4th. - Sunday. Up at 6 AM. Drove south to North Bay. Arrived in time to attend Sunday School and morning service at Faith Chapel. We left North Bay in the afternoon and drove to Ottawa where we spent the night.

August 5th. - Up at 6 AM. We drove through to Montreal and to the lumber yard. Roger and I worked on making a list of supplies for the church at Ivugivik.

August 6th. - Roger's men and I worked hard all day, building crates and packing them full. We completed the job late tonight. I gave Roger a $10,000.00 deposit cheque. He will deliver the material to the Harbour tomorrow. I phoned the shipping company and they will ship the cargo and send me a bill later.

August 7th. - Started to drive home early, and arrived in South Porcupine late, tired but happy.

September 2nd. to 17th., 1985 - We left South Porcupine in our motor home and drove to Montreal with many meetings enroute. Now it's time for our fall Inuit Bible Conference at Broughton Island, N.W.T.

September 18th. - I had asked Graydon Meek, Larry Sault and Keith Spillenaar, my nephew, to come and help teach. We met at the Montreal Dorval airport and we flew north in Nordair's 737 jet. Frobisher Bay was closed in fog. We flew on to Hall's Beach and unloaded a lot of cargo. We flew back to Frobisher Bay, but could not land because of the fog, so we returned to Montreal.

September 19th. - The weather has improved at Frobisher Bay. We flew north from Montreal to Frobisher Bay, intending to change planes and fly on to Broughton Island. The weather was unflyable at Broughton Island so we had to stay at Frobisher Bay.

September 20th. - At Frobisher Bay. Zero degrees C and snowing. We were airborne at 5:45 AM. The weather was too bad to land at Broughton Island, so we flew on north to Pond Inlet where cargo was unloaded. Then we flew south to Clyde River where some passengers got off. We tried to land at Broughton Island but were unable so we flew back to Frobisher Bay. Had a good service in a home here.

September 21st. - At Frobisher Bay. A few people gathered in the home where we are staying. We had a good Bible Study this forenoon. A Twin Otter plane will try to fly to Broughton Island. We all boarded the plane in the early afternoon and landed at Broughton Island in very bad weather.

The church was packed full for the evening service. After I preached a message from the Word, we had a great time of prayer.

September 22nd. - Sunday at Broughton Island. After an early prayer meeting, Graydon Meek brought a powerful message in the morning service. After lunch, the church was packed for an afternoon service, when Brother Larry Sault preached. Quite a few received the Baptism of the Holy Spirit. We moved to the community hall for the evening service. After I brought the message, many Inuits gathered for a time of prayer and seeking the Lord. Some were saved, others healed and a few more were filled with the Holy Spirit.

September 23rd. - At the Inuit Leaders Bible Conference in

Broughton Island, N.W.T. Three great meetings today. I taught in the morning session on "The Holy Spirit", and Graydon Meek preached in the evening service, followed by a great time of prayer at the altar. We also had a water baptismal service, as part of the evening service.

September 24th. - Broughton Island. Conducted two good Bible teachings this morning and then packed up and flew to Frobisher Bay. A large crowd gathered in Mosesee's home for an evening service which lasted till 10:30.

September 25th. - At Frobisher Bay. Graydon Meek, Larry Sault, Annie Tertiluk and I had a good talk with Mosesee and Kuduluk over a disagreement. A reconciliation was achieved. A very good service from 5 to 6 PM and then I flew to Montreal where my wife Tyyne and son Daniel met me at the airport at 11:30 PM.

September 26th. - In our motor home in Montreal. I answered many letters and brought our Harvest Field book work up to date.

September 27th. - We left Montreal and drove to Cornwall. Crossed the U.S. border and drove to Watertown, N.Y.

September 28th. - From Watertown, we drove to Auburn, N.Y. We parked at the Assembly of God church where Rev. Persad is pastor. Prepared for tomorrow's services.

September 29th. - In Auburn, New York at the Assembly of God Church. I shared some of my experiences in the open session of Sunday School, and preached in the morning service. Pastor Sonny Persad took us to his home for dinner. A great service tonight. I brought a message from the Word and showed slides of the missionary work in the Arctic. We had a great time of prayer around the altar as many sought the Lord

September 30th. to October 3rd. Travelled to Cape Coral, Florida.

October 4th., 1985 to February 12th., 1986. In Florida. Kept busy with Harvest Field office work, monthly newsletters, meetings in many different churches, groups and the Full Gospel Business Men's Banquets.

Left: Betsy Kudluarjuk Etidloie and Anautaq from Wakeham Bay.

Below: An elderly Inuit woman.

Bottom: Timothy with a Buelga whale.

Left: Larry Sault at Quartaq

Below: After the wedding at Frobisher Bay.

Bottom: An Inuit meeting at Quartaq.

Left: Inuit lady singing a solo at Quartaq.

Below: Inuit gentleman giving his testimony before water baptism.

Bottom: Arctic char drying in the sun.

Top: We baptized these three Inuit people in a bath tub at Spence Bay.

Bottom: At Grise Fiord, North West Territories, Canada's most northern Inuit community.

Chapter 9

The People Dedicated the House of God

II Chronicles 7:5 "And king Solomon offered a sacrifice of twenty and two thousand oxen, and a hundred and twenty thousand sheep: SO THE KING AND ALL THE PEOPLE DEDICATED THE HOUSE OF GOD."

February 13th., 1986. - It was time to dedicate the new church at Quaqtaq. I flew from Fort Myers, Florida to Montreal. It's cold here compared to Florida.

February 14th. - From Montreal, I flew to Fort Chimo on the south end of Ungava Bay. I had a good time of fellowship in the Anglican minister's home, Rev. Appliee and Lucy Napartuk. I stayed with them overnight.

February 15th. - In Air Inuit's Twin Otter plane, we flew to Payne Bay, then on to Quaqtaq. I visited a few homes including the Anglican minister's. Jim and Lena White of Sarnia came to Quaqtaq a few days earlier to hold special meetings. They are greatly appreciated in all these Inuit settlements. This is Saturday and the dedication service is tomorrow. But the people insisted on a service in the old church. A good number attended and when I gave the altar call, three fine Inuits stepped out to receive Jesus as Saviour. Many others came to seek the Lord.

February 16th. - Sunday. The dedication of the new church was set for 2 PM, but a great number gathered for Sunday morning service at 9:30 AM. Rev. Jim White preached a powerful message and many came forward to pray at the altar.

2 PM. What a great day for the dedication of the fine new church building. This large auditorium was packed full, with many standing at the back. White school teachers and nurses came, and many from the Anglican Church. God blessed in a wonderful way as the Holy Spirit's power descended upon us. Our people were weeping for joy, that God had given them this new church building. After the dedication service, I challenged the people to come forward and dedicate themselves - for service to the Lord. Many responded, committing their lives to the service of King Jesus.

It was almost time for the evening service when we finished the dedication service. I preached on the soon coming of King Jesus - to catch His bride away. Again, we had a great time of rejoicing and thanksgiving.

Some came forward for salvation and healing as well as the Baptism of the Holy Spirit. God did not deny them.

February 17th. - Dawned clear and very cold. The Air Inuit plane flew me to Fort Chimo where I boarded the Nordair 737 jet for Montreal. In Montreal my motel room was $37.00.

February 18th. - From Montreal, I flew to Boston, Washington, Atlanta and to Fort Myers and home. I was tired but rejoicing in "another mission accomplished".

February 19th. to March 11th./86 - Busy as usual.

March 12th., 1986 - I invited Larry Sault of Hagersville, Ont. and Rev. Ross Maracle of Deseronto, Ont. to teach at our Inuit Bible Conference to be held at Ivugivik, Quebec, where we had built a fine church to the glory of God. Peter Anilik is our pastor there. I flew Eastern Airways jet to Montreal.

March 13th. - Larry Sault and I flew to Great Whale River. We stayed with Willie Kumarluk. Our Christians here, obtained a small building to hold services in. A good number requested an evening service. God blessed and I brought the message from the Word of God.

March 14th. - At Great Whale River on the east shore of the Hudson Bay. Forty five degrees below zero. We flew north to Povungnituk. Had a great service in a home. The Christians were encouraged to trust in the faithfulness of God.

March 15th. - At Povungnituk. I got up at 5 AM, made and ate breakfast. Had to ride on a skidoo to the airstrip about one mile from town, but it seemed like ten miles because it was so cold. We flew to Ivugivik in time for a great service in a packed church - which marked the beginning of our Bible Conference.

March 16th. - Sunday. Many of our Full Gospel Fellowship Inuit pastors and church workers had already flown in for the dedication of this new church building and for the Bible Conference. The building was packed for the morning service, as Larry Sault brought a great message from the Word. At 2 PM, the church was more than packed full, so many had to stand in the back and in the aisle while the children came and sat on the floor around the platform.

God gave us a precious time in His presence as I brought the dedication message. These wonderful Inuit people rejoiced, even with tears of joy flowing down their faces - at the good hand of the Lord making it possible to have a church building to worship in. Another wonderful evening service was held with a great altar service as so many folk came to seek the Lord.

March 17th. - Ivugivik. A very cold day. Larry Sault, Udjualuk Etidloie and our pastor from Cape Dorset and Peter the pastor and I took turns in four teaching sessions and the evening service. Three Inuits came forward for salvation. We also baptized five candidates in water.

March 18th. - Ross Maracle arrived with Denis Pringle who took videos of the Bible Conference. They had been delayed with bad weather, but now were here to help teach.

When I gave the altar call after the evening service, four more came to receive Jesus as Saviour. Peter and I baptized four more who had previously committed their lives to Jesus.

March 19th. - At Ivugivik Bible Conference. Another great day of teaching as Ross, Larry and I alternated in the teaching sessions. Ross Maracle preached a powerful message in the evening service followed by the response of a great number of Inuits who came forward for prayer.

March 20th. - Ivugivik. A terrific blizzard raged all day long, and the temperatures were very cold; but the weather did not hinder the conference at all. The three of us alternated in teaching and Larry Sault preached on "Healing". We prayed for a number of Inuits who were not well in body.

March 21st. to 24th. God honoured the teaching of His Word. More souls were saved in each service. 53 Inuits had flown in from other settlements, plus the ones from this assembly. This is the largest Bible Conference yet. We closed with a communion service and one lady from Sugluk was baptized in our second baptismal service.

March 25th. - The Inuit Bible Conference is over. But a raging blizzard all day prevented planes from flying. We had another great service tonight with Larry Sault preaching to a very good crowd.

March 26th. - At Ivugivik, Quebec. The Twin Otter turbo jet had to make two flights to Sugluk, with full loads from the conference. At 5 PM, the plane returned and we flew south to Povungnituk, then on to Great Whale River.

March 27th. - At Great Whale River. We flew with Nordair to Montreal. Larry Sault flew on to Toronto. Ross Maracle and Denis Pringle had their car here, and drove to Deseronto. I stayed at the Airport Inn for $37.00.

March 28th. - Flew south to New York, Atlanta and Fort Myers, Florida, Dan met me and drove me home.

March 31st. to April 15th., 1986 Had a few meetings enroute. Souls were saved. We shared what God is doing in the Canadian Arctic. I showed slides of the north. Arrived home in South Porcupine on April 28th.

May 26th., 1986 - At South Porcupine, Ontario. On my last visits to Igloolik and Frobisher Bay, N.W.T., I was requested to send materials to build churches in both of these settlements. I had promised to meet these requests - with the help of the Lord. I, in myself, did not know how we could build two churches in one year. But since this is not my work, but the work of the Lord, I knew we could trust the Lord to meet all our needs.

While I was conducting meetings in Apsley, Ontario, I mentioned the need of a church building in Igloolik.

Pastor Ward Trotter's brother, Sanford Trotter said he would cut logs in his bush, saw them into lumber and supply the lumber for the church at Igloolik. Praise the Lord! So today, my wife Tyyne and I drove south in our motor home to North Bay. We had some business to look after there and then drove on to Huntsville where we stopped for the night.

May 27th. - At Huntsville. We drove to Bancroft to see Dan Freeman who has the lumber yard and trucks. While I was at Apsley, Pastor Trotter had phoned Dan Freeman about trucking the lumber from Apsley to Montreal in time to load it on the ship. We had a nice visit with Dan Freeman and he assured us that his men would deliver the Lumber to Montreal.

We drove through to Ottawa to visit our son David, his wife Shirley and their daughter Shelley Lee.

May 28th. - In Ottawa. We continued to Montreal. At Beaver Lumber, Roger the owner, and I worked on the list of materials needed for the two churches. Sanford Trotter had supplied most of the lumber needed for the church at Igloolik, and I had a list of it all. So now we just needed the plywood for the flooring, plywood for the roof, insulation, electrical wiring, nails, an oil heater, windows and doors, etc. Then we needed the total materials for the Frobisher Bay church. We also had to include some furniture for the living quarters.

Roger and his wife were living in a mansion of a home. But now he bought a condo and had too much furniture. He drove us to his home and picked out two sofas, three large stuffed chairs, three end tables, etc. All these Roger donated to the parsonage at Frobisher Bay.

May 30th. - All these items had to be crated, after we built the many crates for the supplies and furniture. We worked hard from early morning to late at night.

June 1st., 1986 - Sunday. In Montreal we attended the French Pentecostal Church this morning. Then we drove through to Ottawa where we attended the Woodvale Pentecostal Church for the evening service, with our son David and his wife Shirley.

June 2nd. to 3rd. - Drove north to North Bay and Kirkland Lake, then back to South Porcupine.

June 14th. - I officiated at the wedding of another Laotian couple, who were friends with the Laotian Boat people that we brought over.

**Eccleslastes 3:1 "To everything there is a season, and
a time to every purpose under the heaven."**

June 27th. - Having felt the need of younger workers to
carry on the missionary work of Harvest Field, we approached
the president of the Full Gospel Fellowship, David Bailey to be
responsible for this work. He suggested that since Larry Sault
had been up north and helped to teach, he might be the one
to carry it on. We agreed and Larry and his wife Sonja drove
up from Hagersville, Ontario with their half ton truck. After I
explained the details of the work, we loaded the office equipment of Harvest Field into the truck and they drove south.
Now it was Larry Sault's responsibility to write up and print as
well as mail the monthly Harvest Field news letter.

June 28th. - We had a good garage sale and sold most of
our belongings which we did not need. We loaded our personal
things in our motor home and started our trip south. We arrived in Temagami late, so we parked for the night.

June 29th. - From Temagami, we drove south past Toronto
to Kitchener, Ontario to our friends Mel and Clara Harmer.

June 30th. In Kitchener. We phoned around to many real estate agencies to rent a two bedroom apartment. We checked
on a few but did not rent.

July 1st. 1986 - We rented a two bedroom at 550 Strasburg
Road, Kitchener. I paid two months rent and then we drove
north.

July 2nd. to 4th. - Worked on getting things ready for another garage sale.

July 5th. - A big garage sale and many people came to buy.
We sold the remainder of the things we did not need.

July 9th. - I rented a U Haul truck. Many came to help us load
up. We towed our Golf Volkswagen behind the truck and
drove to Kirkland Lake.

July 10th. - From Kirkland Lake, we drove to Kitchener. I
phoned our friend Monty Oakes and told him that we had arrived. He employs many men in his plant and sent three men
over to help us unload. So, here we are living in Kitchener,
Ontario.

August 7th., 1986 - At Kitchener. Larry Sault, Jim Lee and I
made arrangements for our fall Inuit Bible Conference to be
held at Payne Bay, on Ungava Bay in northern Quebec.

Monty Oakes drove me to the Toronto airport, where I met
Larry and Jim. We flew to Montreal, then north to Fort Chimo
on Nordair, and to Payne Bay on Air Inuit. I shared the Word
in the evening service to a good crowd, as many Inuit had already flown in from other settlements. A good altar service
followed.

August 8th. to 11th. Larry, Jim and I alternated in teaching the two morning sessions, two afternoon sessions and the evening public services. God blessed in a wonderful way, as souls were saved, some outstanding healings and others received the Baptism of the Holy Spirit.

August 12th. - At Payne Bay, Quebec. A phone call from Frobisher Bay requested me to come and solve a problem regarding the lot on which the church was to be built. The materials had already come and Udjualuk Etidloie was in charge of the building project. So I flew to Fort Chimo and on to Frobisher Bay, while Larry and Jim carried on at the Bible Conference.

August 13th. - At Frobisher Bay. We visited the town office and I signed the necessary papers for our building site and arranged to have the lot prepared to start building.

August 14th. to 19th - At Frobisher Bay. Delays - delays - delays: to get trucks to haul gravel, to get the electrical company to install temporary power lines, to haul our church crates and bundles from the beach to the church site. Finally everything was in order to begin building.

August 20th. - I flew to Fort Chimo - tired out.

August 21st. - Larry Sault and Jim Lee flew in from Payne Bay after completing the Bible Conference there. We flew to Montreal and Toronto. Tyyne and Dan met me and we drove home to Kitchener.

August 28th. - My Wife Tyyne is from Finland, so we decided to fly to Finland and visit some of her relatives there and conduct gospel services. Monty Oakes drove us to the Toronto airport. We flew Air Canada to Montreal and then changed over to FinnAir.

August 29th. We arrived in Finland at 5 AM. Toronto time, which is 12 noon here in Helsinki. Some of Tyyne's relatives met us at the airport and drove us to Pieksamake, a town north of Helsinki.

August 30th. to September 12th., 1986 - We met many of Tyyne's relatives. They announced a family reunion and people came from many parts of Finland. About 80 people came. We took advantage of the occasion and held a gospel meeting. My messages were interpreted, whereas Tyyne was right at home preaching in her own language.

Relatives drove us around to many different towns and cities where we conducted services nearly every night; sometimes in churches, other times in homes. Many hearts were touched and some accepted Jesus as Saviour.

September 13th. - It's time to leave Finland and return home. Relatives took us to the Helsinki airport. It was a clear day and we could see Sweden, Norway, Iceland, Greenland

and the Labrador coast. We landed at Montreal, changed planes and flew on to Toronto, where Daniel was waiting for us and drove us home to Kitchener.

October 3rd. to 27th., 1986 - Left Kitchener - arrived Cape Coral, Florida. Had meetings enroute. God blessed. Altars were filled night after night. Souls were saved, the sick healed and recommitments made as the Holy Spirit spoke and people surrendered in obedience.

November 27th to December 3rd., 1986 - Cape Coral, Florida. I flew north to Timmins and then drove to Kirkland Lake, Ontario where I shared in the Full Gospel Business Men's Fellowship Banquet. A few fine men and women came forward for prayer. Some had been church members for years, but had never been "born again". Some miracles of salvation and healing took place, as testified to later.

Glen and Grace Adams, pastor of the "Living Faith" church, asked me to be their 50th church anniversary speaker, for both morning and evening service, as the church started 50 years ago when I was the Pastor. God blessed and touched hearts as many people came to the altar in obedience to God's call.

St. Luke 19:10 "For the Son of man is come to seek and to save that which was lost."

February 4th., 1987 - Tyyne and Dan drove me to the Fort Myers, Florida airport, I flew north to Montreal.

February 5th. - In Montreal. I flew in Nordair's 737 jet to Great Whale River on the Hudson Bay. Willie Kumarluk met me and took me to his home, where we conducted a good Bible teaching.

February 6th. - Flew north to the new Inuit village of Umiujaq. We flew over thousands of caribou migrating north along the east coast of Hudson Bay. Noah, the head man of this village showed me the building for us to use for a church, in exchange for the lumber and building supplies we had shipped to Great Whale River. I stayed in Charlie and Eva Sappa's home, where many people gathered for a Bible Study and prayer meeting.

February 7th. - I had a good talk with Noah about the Grace of God in the salvation message. Eva Sappa was on the local radio preaching the good news of the Gospel.

We met in Billy's home for a Bible teaching on "Having the whole armour of God on." Ephesians 6:10-18.

February 8th. - Sunday at Umiujaq. Thirty six degrees below zero plus the wind chill factor. Glen and Lizzie wanted the next service in their home. We celebrated "the Lord's Supper" here this morning

It was a precious time as we remembered the suffering and death of our Lord and Saviour Jesus Christ. Our evening service was in Charlie and Eva Sappa's home. A great crowd gathered in.

We built a tank and had it ready for the Water Baptismal Service. Seven candidates followed the Lord in Water Baptism. One Inuit woman, I would judge to be about thirty years old, attended her very first gospel service. She asked many questions and when she received Bible answers, she and two others accepted Jesus as Saviour.

February 9th. - At Umiujaq, Quebec. Forty five degrees below zero. The plane arrived late and we flew back to Great Whale River.

February 10th. - Another cold day with frosty, biting winds. Had another profitable Bible Study in Willie's home.

February 11th. - At Great Whale River, Quebec on the east coast of Hudson Bay. Willie and I had a good time of Bible Study and prayer, before he left for work. The 737 jet arrived and I flew back to Montreal, then on to Fort Myers, Florida on U.S. Air.

March 26th., 1987 - Left Cape Coral, Florida and travelled northward. Stayed in Campers Resorts each night. Met some very fine people and was able to share the gospel with them. Gave out dozens of the "Voice" magazines.

April 15th., 1987 - Arrived in Kitchener to a huge pile of mail waiting for attention. We thank God for His protecting care as we travel.

Business at Frobisher Bay required our attention, also a wedding.

May 5th., 1987 - Kitchener, Ontario. Up at 4:20 AM and drove to Toronto airport where I met Rev. George Mallory. We flew to Montreal, intending to fly north to Frobisher Bay, but the weather was not good at all so we stayed at the Airport Inn where we had a good time of Bible reading and prayer.

May 6th. - In Montreal. We flew to Frobisher Bay where Larry Sault and Jim Lee met us. We held a business meeting in our Full Gospel Church parsonage. God met with us and gave us wisdom to deal with the situation.

May 7th. - Cold and snowing here at Frobisher Bay, N.W.T. on Baffin Island. We contacted the bank to change the names of the signing officers of our "Faith Alive" Church. Also a letter was drafted and sent to the Town Hall about this Harvest Field church property. I visited one home.

St. John 2:1-2 "And the third day there was a marriage in Cana of Galilee; and the mother of

**Jesus was there: and both Jesus was called,
and His disciples, to the marriage."**

May 8th. - At Frobisher Bay, N.W.T., Baffin Island. A most beautiful wedding took place here in our "Faith Alive" church. It was requested that it be a quiet wedding, with only a few chosen people attending. I officiated as Brian and Rebecca made their vows to each other. God's blessing was implored upon this fine couple, as they serve the Lord together.

May 9th. At Frobisher Bay. Up at 2:30 AM. as our flight was to leave early. But it was delayed till 7:15 AM. We flew to Montreal and on to Toronto where Tyyne and Dan met us with our motor home. We travelled to Apsley, Ontario where Rev. Ward Trotter is pastor.

May 10th. - Sunday. Two wonderful services here in the Apsley Community Church. A number of people came forward for prayer. God met us and touched hearts.

May 11th. to 20th. - We travelled to Gooderham, Bancroft, Palmer Rapids, Ottawa, North Bay, Kirkland Lake and South Porcupine before returning to Kitchener, Ontario.

More wedding bells are ringing! Phone calls from the Arctic requesting me to fly north to officiate at five weddings.

August 6th., 1987 - Starting on my trip north, I flew from Toronto to Montreal where I stayed at the Airport Inn for $37.00.

August 7th. - At Montreal. Was up at 5:30 AM. Flew to Fort Chimo on "Canadian" 737 jet. Then to Payne Bay on Air Inuit's Twin Otter plane. I stayed in Tomassie's home. Some of our Inuit Christians came over for a good visit.

August 8th. Payne Bay, which is on Ungava Bay in Northern Quebec. Some of the Inuit hunters arrived with three big walrus. I filled out wedding forms and had a rehearsal. Had a very good evening service in the church. When I gave the altar call, many came up for prayer and seeking God.

August 9th. I officiated at the wedding of Daniel and Mary. Afterward the chairs in the church were stacked up, cardboard laid out on the floor, and the women brought in a lot of food for the wedding feast. And what a feast it was! Walrus, seal, Canada goose, caribou, whale, etc.

August 10th. - At Payne Bay. I flew to Quaqtaq. Stayed in Brother Charlie's home. Matthew, one of our Inuit Christian men came to see me. He said, "Do you remember when you first flew to Payne Bay years ago? I was your interpreter. After the meetings, I offered to take your suitcases and things to your plane on the river ice with my dog team. I charged you $10.00 for that trip. That was before I was converted. I felt so bad about that and now I want to make it right. Here is

$20.00 to to repay the $10.00 plus interest." Well - praise the Lord!

We had a most wonderful service in our new church this evening. A spirit of praise and worship prevailed.

August 11th. - At Quaqtaq. A few came over to Charlie's house to visit me asking for prayer for jobs and healings. Another great service in the church this evening.

August 12th. - I flew from Quaqtaq to Wakeham Bay. Charlie, the mayor of Wakeham Bay, and I went over the plans for a wedding. A very good evening service in the church here. I preached on the "soon return of Jesus". Many came to the altar to pray.

August 13th. - At Wakeham Bay, on the shores of Hudson Strait in northern Quebec. Now, there are three couples to be married, and the church is too small for the large crowd expected. So the weddings were held in the large school gym.

Charlie, the mayor and Alasie were the first to be married. Then Tommy, Charlie's brother, and Ulaayu were second. Next was the police officer, Emataluk and Paijougie. A very large crowd filled the gym. Before I performed the weddings, we had a good gospel service, with singing, testimonies, a short gospel message and prayer.

Many of the women left the gym, but in a few minutes returned with many good things to eat.

August 14th. A larger church building is needed here. We built this one in 1979 and now it's too small. We thank the Lord for the many people saved here in the past eight years. The men and I worked on plans for the new church most of the day. A great Bible teaching this evening in our Full Gospel Church.

August 15th. - At Wakeham Bay. I visited a few homes. Had prayer with a few sick folk, who appreciated my visits. Studied and prayed for tomorrow's services.

August 16th. - Sunday. God blessed in both morning and evening services, as I brought forth the Word of God. The altar was filled after both services. I thank God for the spiritual hunger in these Inuit hearts.

August 17th. - At Wakeham Bay. The plane flights were cancelled because of bad weather. Another good Bible Study tonight.

August 18th. - The weather is clearing. The plane arrived and we flew to Quaqtaq, but could not land because of extremely poor visibility. We flew on to Payne Bay. The folk here requested a service in our church tonight. God blessed and many came to the altar, with tears of repentance flowing down their faces, as they accepted Jesus as their Saviour.

August 19th. - At Payne Bay. I flew on to Aupaluk. I prepared for and performed the marriage of Willie and Lolly, after we had a brief gospel service. A wedding feast followed which everyone enjoyed.

August 20th. - At Aupaluk, Quebec on Ungava Bay. I had ordered all the church building supplies to come here on this summer's supply ship. The ship had come in and unloaded just before I arrived. We checked over the many bundles of lumber, plywood and crates. One bundle of 2 x 12 floor joist was missing. We checked among the government housing supplies and found our missing bundle.

A great service of thanksgiving to the Lord was held this evening, as the people knew they would soon have their own church to worship in.

August 21st. Aupaluk. I flew out to Fort Chimo on Air Inuit and on Canadian to Montreal and Toronto. Another mission accomplished, for which we give all the honour and glory to Jesus.

September 17th., 1987 Kitchener, Ontario. I received a letter from the Quebec government, informing me that some of the information given in the wedding of Daniel and Mary at Payne Bay on August 9th., was incorrect, and advised me to provide the necessary changes. This means that I must fly north to Payne Bay to find out the correct answers. So this evening I flew from Toronto to Montreal where I stayed at the Airport Inn.

September 18th. - Montreal. Up at 5:30 AM., had breakfast and took the shuttle service to the airport. Quite a few whites and Inuits were coming in. Just a few seats from where I was sitting there was a young Inuit couple with an older Inuit who had been in the Montreal Hospital. This older Inuit man fell over and died right there. A nurse who was in the waiting room pronounced him dead.

I flew north to Fort Chimo. The Anglican minister Appliee, met me at the airport and took me to his home. A few people gathered in and we had a good Bible Study. One Inuit girl about 20 years old, accepted Jesus as Saviour.

September 19th. - Fort Chimo. Freezing ice on the water. Appliee took me to the airport. I flew in Air Inuit's Twin Otter turbo jet to Payne Bay. I contacted the relatives of Daniel and Mary who I had married on August 9th., 1987. I found out that Mary had given her adopted parent's names. As many hundreds of Inuit babies are born, many of them were already spoken for before the baby was born. So the baby never knew its real mother. I was able to get the correct information for the government files.

September 20th. - Sunday at Payne Bay. Many Inuits gathered in church for the morning worship. God blessed in a special way, and six came forward for prayer and various needs. A larger crowd attended the evening service, as some came in from camping. Twelve came for prayer, some with tears of repentance trickling down their faces. God does pardon sin and gives peace to them who truly repent.

September 21st. to 22nd. - I flew to Aupaluk. Our people gave me a nice home to stay in alone, where I could have peace and quietness to pray and study. A good crowd gathered in for the evening services, as I expounded from the Word of God. Many came to the altar for a fresh touch from the hand of God. I had a good chance to visit in quite a few homes. These Inuit people really appreciated my visits.

September 23rd. - At Aupaluk. I visited a few homes and had prayer. The Air Inuit plane came in early. Eva, the school teacher, took me to the airstrip in her half ton truck. I flew to Fort Chimo in time to board the 737 Canadian jet to Montreal.

September 24th. - In Montreal I had a good opportunity to witness at the Airport Motel. Flew to Toronto, drove home to Kitchener.

October 2nd., 1987 - Daniel, Tyyne and I packed things in our motor home and drove south. We crossed the U.S. border at Lewiston where we visited my brother Matthew and wife Rita.

October 13th. - We arrived at Cape Coral, Florida. Met many wonderful people enroute and had good opportunities to share the gospel and give out gospel literature.

October 13th. to April 4th., 1988. - Had some wonderful speaking engagements this winter here in Florida. We thank the Lord for many souls saved. Now we are leaving Cape Coral, Florida on our trip north to Canada.

April 4th. to April 12th. - A few good meetings enroute. God blessed and souls were saved. We crossed the Ontario border at Windsor today at 10 AM. Glad to be back in Canada.

Evangelistic Missionary Trip to the High Arctic 1988

May 3rd. to 15th., 1988 - Tyyne and I left Toronto early this morning and drove north in our motor home. Our first stop was in Sudbury. Then we proceeded to Sault Ste. Marie the following day, and on up to Kirkland Lake on May 5th. Much mail was waiting for us at Grace, our daughter's home. There were many bills to be paid. On May 10th., I made a business trip to Cochrane, then on to Hearst and return. Much more mail arrived which kept me busy answering until May 14th.

During this time I prepared for the trip to the Arctic. I packed my heavy parka, big flight boots and heavy underwear. I drew $7000. out of the bank and after paying my flight to

Frobisher Bay, N.W.T., I took the rest in travellers cheques. Right here I want to thank each and every one of you who contributed to the expenses of this trip. Also, for those who faithfully prayed for us. God answered your prayers in a wonderful way. Each one who had any part in this trip will be rewarded accordingly.

May 16th. - Cecil Stearns of Timmins drove me to the airport where I took the Air Canada flight to Montreal, Quebec. Our Inuit pastor at Cape Dorset, N.W.T. phoned me to order quite a large amount of supplies to be shipped on the boat this summer. This took most of the day of the 17th.

May 18th. - I flew north on Canadian Airways to Frobisher Bay. At the air terminal, I was so glad to see Jim Lee of our Full Gospel Fellowship and Wayne Moore of the Pentecostal Assemblies as well as Udjualuk of the Cape Dorset Full Gospel Church. That night was our first service in the Arctic in our Full Gospel Church. The Lord was present to touch each one of our hearts.

May 19th. - I purchased tickets for Udjualuk and I. We went by Canadian Air 737 Jet to Nanisivik on the northern end of Baffin Island. A taxi drove us the 18 miles to Arctic Bay. Services were held here at the Full Gospel Church each night to May 24th. We thank the Lord for souls saved and sick bodies healed by the power of God. I also performed a lovely wedding for a young Inuit couple. There is quite a lot of snow on Baffin Island, which is approximately 1000 miles long! It snowed again on May 25th. as we drove to Nanisivik where we held a service in the chapel at the mine site. Quite a good attendance and many responded to the altar call for salvation, healing and rededication.

May 26th. - I purchased tickets for Udjualuk and I to fly north to Resolute on Cornwallis Island. The weather was beautiful, minus five degrees. It's Kenn Boreck Airways that goes to many of these high Arctic villages, using the twin Otter plane. We were able to visit quite a number of homes here. Many Inuits accepted Jesus as their Saviour. We had to keep in touch with the airway office to find out when the next plane flew north to the last Eskimo settlement, nearest to the North Pole, Grise Fiord on Ellsmere Island.

May 29th. - We received word to hurry to the airport as a plane was leaving immediately. At Grise Fiord, the Anglican Church minister met us. We would be staying in his home and preaching in his church.

My last trip here to Grise Fiord was in 1982. I did not know a soul. It was a difficult time. That's the time when I was out about a quarter of a mile east of the village taking pictures and walking slowly back to the village with two big polar bears beside me! I was able to visit many homes and witness to the saving power of Jesus Christ.

Now the people are more friendly. Udjualuk and I were able to minister to the Inuits. We found a real openness and hunger for God's Word, rather than the tradition of man. God answered prayer and a number of precious souls turned to Jesus!

Incidentally, all fresh fruit and vegetables, milk and bread must be flown in. Prices are as follows: Bread - $3.89, litre of milk - $4.98, dozen eggs - $5.89, one pork chop - $6.18, 7.15, 7.80 and 8.20.

We were to fly out on June 2nd., but a terrific snow blizzard blew all day long so no planes could fly.

June 3rd., 1988 - We were able to fly to Pond Inlet. North of the Arctic Circle, the sun never sets all summer long! This makes it difficult to sleep. Wherever we travelled, we were told that this spring was the earliest on record, in fact a month and a half earlier than other years. Although the temperatures were down to minus ten, it usually was up to zero or plus five some days.

We had very good services at Pond Inlet. We had been there quite often in the past twelve years. I was asked to preach in the Parish Hall and Anglican Church. Many came forward when the invitation was given. The Holy Spirit touched many hearts and souls were saved. After the Sunday morning service, I thought it would be nice to have a good Sunday dinner at the new lodge built since my last visit. There was no menu. I received a plate with French fries, two small pieces of steak, possibly caribou, each steak was about one inch wide and three inches long and about an eighth of an inch thick! I had coffee and a small piece of pie, all this for $25.00. I apologize for using some of your missionary offering for this meal. Please forgive me. All in all, the Lord blessed at Pond Inlet and a great work was done in many hearts.

June 6th. - Udjualuk and I flew to Igloolik where we had built a Full Gospel church in 1986. We stayed at our pastor's home, Peter Awa. Again, God blessed in the services each night. Udjualuk and I took turns preaching. We had Bible Studies in homes; we witnessed to the grace of God which has appeared to all men. We thank God for our faithful pastors who are preaching the gospel and doing a great work for the Lord all through the Arctic.

June 14th. - We flew to Clyde River which is on the east coast of Baffin Island. I had visited there once before but found little interest in the Lord. However, this trip was different. We found people with open hearts and a hunger for the Word. We had a very good meeting in one of the homes and were able to minister to many of these precious Inuit people.

Three accepted Jesus. It was snowing and blowing during our stay.

June 16th. - We flew to Broughton Island, which is off the east coast of Baffin Island toward Greenland. We had a very good service here in the Full Gospel Church, followed by a good response to our altar call where we prayed with a good number of people. One of our young men is the second in command at the housing office. Another is the head man for the huge territory park in the Broughton Island office. One of our ladies is the head of social services. She asked us to go with her to her office and pray for God's presence to rest upon all the problem people who came to her office for help. We had a good prayer meeting there. We could only spend one night here as the First Air plane would fly to Pangnirtung tomorrow.

June 17th. This was our first visit to Pangnirtung with a population of 1200 people. Not knowing anyone here, we took our room and meals at the Hotel at $300. per day for both of us. Naturally our stay here was very short! We were able to visit many homes and had reading and prayer with some. The good seed was sown in many hearts. Questions were answered from the Bible and a few prayed the sinner's prayer. A message over the radio welcomed us to Pangnirtung.

June 20th. - We flew to another new village called Lake Harbour. It's a beautiful place built on the side of a fiord. Some members of a family here visited at Cape Dorset and attended Udjualuk's church service. We found a welcome here in this home. He videotaped the service at Cape Dorset and we showed this tape to many people in most of the villages. We had many good opportunities to witness to people here, many who asked questions regarding eternal life. We prayed with a few souls for salvation.

June 22nd. - The First Air plane flew us to Frobisher Bay in time for the evening service. A nice group gathered as we preached and a good altar call followed as God touched those precious hearts.

June 23rd. - I flew on to Montreal, Udjualuk would spend a few days in Frobisher Bay. Brother and Sister Solonen met me at the Dorval airport. They drove me to the Montreal General Hospital where one of our Eskimo women was very ill. Her operation was too late and she was stitched up again. We had prayer and peace touched her heart. She said, "All my fears have gone. I now have God's peace in my heart and will accept God's will for me".

June 24th. - I arrived back in Timmins. Cecil Stearns met me at the airport and took me to his home. His wife had prepared a wonderful meal. I drove on to Kirkland Lake where Tyyne was waiting for me.

June 25th. - We started our drive south and stopped at Barrie overnight. We arrived back in Kitchener on June 26th. The expenses of this trip came to $6649.93, It was well worth it as souls were saved for eternity.

During the last few days with Udjualuk he mentioned that he received calls from villages further west. He asked, "Can we plan on another trip later on to visit more new Eskimo settlements in the central Arctic"? We are praying that once again the Lord will meet this need.

September 14th., 1988 - On my previous visit to Ivugivik, Quebec, I was asked by Pastor Peter to visit a young couple who were living together but not married. I had a nice visit with them, until I suggested that they ought to get married. I was told in no uncertain terms to mind my own business.

Now I've received a phone call from Ivugivik to come up at once to marry this same couple. They attended our Full Gospel Church and had accepted Jesus as their Saviour. Now they know they can not live together as they had before, so requested I come up right away to perform their wedding.

So this morning, here in Kitchener I got up at 4 AM. The Airport van took me to the Toronto airport. I flew to Montreal, then to Great Whale River. Glen Calvin met me and I stayed in his home.

September 15th. - In the Air Inuit Twin Otter turbo jet, we flew to Port Harrison, Povungnituk and on north to Ivugivik. Karl Kristensen and Pastor Peter met me, and took me to Lucassie's home to stay. We had a good service here in Lucassie's home, and the Christians were encouraged to "fight the good fight of faith".

September 16th. At Ivugivik, Quebec on the north east point of Hudson Bay. There was a cover of snow over everything this morning. We completed the documents for the wedding. In most of our Arctic weddings, the Christians take advantage of the crowds that attend - with gospel singing, testimonies and short gospel messages. So this was the order of our service tonight. The church was packed full, with many standing at the back. Then I performed the wedding for Novoalia and Nakasok.There was more singing and sharing till after midnight.

September 17th. - At Ivugivik. I visited a few homes and prayed for some sick folk. Had a very good service in our church. Many came to the altar to rededicate themselves to the Lord.

September 18th. - Sunday. Our morning service was from 11 AM to 1:30. God blessed in a wonderful way. My topic was "We have an anchor". I had dinner at Karl Kristensen's home.

There was another great evening service, with a full church. My subject was, "Put on the armour of God." A good altar service followed.

September 19th to 20th. - Three degrees below zero C. Snowing and blowing and no planes flying. Good services in the church both nights as the people gathered to rejoice in the Lord. Some of the Inuit men went out hunting walrus. The Air Inuit plane came in late and I flew to Povungnituk. I stayed at Aeliassie Sutlvaluk's home, and had a late service there.

September 21st. - At Povungnituk. Up at 5 AM. We flew to Port Harrison, Belcher Islands, then to Umiujaq. I stayed with Charlie and Eva Sappa. Many gathered for an evening service and I preached on "The second coming of Jesus". A good time of prayer followed.

September 22nd. At Umiujaq. I visited a few homes. Some accepted Jesus as Saviour. Another great service tonight, as one by one, the Christians testified of the goodness of God upon their lives. The altar was filled after I preached from the Word.

September 23rd. to 25th. - We had services each night. There were adults and young people who surrendered to the Lord, accepting Him as Saviour.

September 26th. At Umiujaq. Flew to Great Whale River, Montreal and on to Toronto and home in Kitchener. Another mission accomplished to the glory of God.

October 3rd., 1988 - Left our condo in Kitchener to travel south. Conducted many meetings here in Ontario. Crossed the U.S. border at Lewiston on October 19th.

October 28th. - We arrived in Cape Coral, Florida after good meetings in different denominational churches and independent groups. Souls were saved.

Luke 13:29 "And they shall come from the east, and from the west, and from the <u>NORTH</u>, and from the south, and shall sit down in the Kingdom of God."

Chapter 10

So Send I You

John 20:21 "As my Father has sent me even so send I
you"
2 Corinthians 10:16 "to preach the gospel in the regions
beyond"

February 13th., 1989. 6.00 AM. Time to rise and shine.
Tyyne got my breakfast ready and Rose Harmer, our daughter,
drove me to the Fort Myers, Florida airport enroute to the
Arctic. By 7.45 PM, I arrived in the Montreal airport. It's cold
here compared to Florida. I had a good chance to witness to a
number of people on the flight to Atlanta, then to New York
and to here. One of the men was a lawyer, another was a
Jewish Rabbi. Both of them as well as others, accepted my
wallet size 1989 calendar with the scripture verses on it.

February 14th. 6.00 AM. Time to get up. At 6.30 PM I am in
Frobisher Bay on Baffin Island. We left Montreal this morning
with a temperature of minus six, and we flew north to Fort
Chimo where it was much colder, then on here to Frobisher
Bay.

I am staying with a family who lived in Cape Dorset. They
were just telling me how I came to their little shack of a house
about 3:00 AM on the 13th of April, 1977. I talked with them
at that time and showed them scriptures until about 5 AM.
when both of them surrendered to the Lord They showed me
a letter I had written them after I returned home in 1977. He
still treasures and keeps it all these years.

At 7:15 PM it is time to go to church. Quite a large crowd
has gathered here in the church building we built in 1987.
We've been singing such lively choruses as *Jesus is Alive,
He's not dead,* and *This is the Day the Lord hath Made.* One of
the Inuit men testified what Jesus has done for him.

It ended at about 10:20 PM following a great service and
altar call. Many came forward for prayer, some for salvation,
some for healing and some for deliverance from bad habits.

February 15th. - It is minus 20 degrees and at 10:30 AM I
went to the Hudson Bay Store and bought a few groceries. I
was told that last week, and for many weeks before, the temperature was more than forty degrees below zero, and now it
is getting mild. Before leaving for the store a young girl, eighteen years old, came and asked if she could surrender to the
Lord. I prayed with her. She also prayed the Sinner's Prayer,

asking Jesus to save her and come into her heart.

This same girl, Nancy, had a good Bible Study this afternoon. She had no Bible, but I gave her one that I had brought with me. She was so interested in reading what the Bible says on sins forgiven through the blood of Jesus Christ and the assurance of salvation.

Quite a few Christians gathered for prayer before the service tonight and what a wonderful time of singing choruses like *Alive, Alive, My Jesus is Alive,* and *When He calls me, I Will Answer, I'll Be Somewhere Working For My Lord.* These are wonderful choruses and they love to sing them in their own Inuit language. The service ended at 9.20, and Udjualuk, the Eskimo pastor who travels with me on these trips preached and many came forward for prayer.

February 16th. - 6:45 AM. It is twenty four degrees below zero. After packing I got a bite of breakfast and went out to the airport. At 9:20 we were at 16,000 feet winging our way to Igloolik. I recognized some of the passengers on the plane as they had attended our services in Frobisher Bay, Arctic Bay and many of the other Inuit settlements.

At 12:05 PM we are at our pastor's home, Peter Awa. It is cold as we are a little more than 200 miles North of the Arctic Circle. Last night it was 44 degrees below zero here, but now it is only thirty three degrees below. There is a very low ceiling and very poor visibility for flying. I am so glad that I am not piloting the plane up here these days in this kind of weather. This afternoon I visited Ian Smith and his wife Gillian. Ian is the principal of the lovely big school here. I met Gillian's brother in a church in Cape Coral, Florida. He asked me to visit his sister and husband up here at Igloolik. The Smith's asked me to come and visit them at their home. It is so bitterly cold to walk any distance. It feels like at least 100 degrees below zero.

We met tonight in the church we built in 1987, one of two we built that year. People sang so well and worshipped the Lord and there was a great response to the altar call. It was a wonderful time of blessing and God gave me real liberty to preach the Word. Now, after the service there is a terrific blizzard raging, the worst of the whole winter and it is bitterly cold.

February 17th. - We had a good time of prayer this morning with Udjualuk and Peter, the Pastor. Peter's wife teaches at the school and the children are in school. Peter is a carpenter as well as a preacher, and is building a house for himself. He has taken time off while we are here.

About 11:40 AM. an Inuit man came to see me. We had a nice visit together. Apparently, it is getting milder and instead of being forty to forty five degrees below zero, it's now only thirty six below and the storm has abated. I can see five dog teams out on the ice a few hundred yards off shore. The Inuits tie them up there when they are not in use. There are from eight to twelve dogs in each team and they are tied there even when the temperature is forty five to fifty degrees below zero. Tonight a number of folk gathered for prayer before the service. Udjualuk preached on the importance of each member in the body of Christ. In spite of the bitterly cold weather, these services are so blessed of God and the warmth of the Holy Spirit is evident as the people worship the Lord. Even the little children came up for prayer.

February 18th. - Elizabeth, the pastor's wife, told me that the first school ever here at Igloolik was in 1960. She was twelve years old then, and now she is teaching the beginner's class. She has been the teacher for a few years.

The spontaneous praise and worship in tonight's service is so warm and inspiring. as the Holy Spirit moves upon the hearts of believers. After I finished speaking, Udjualuk spoke as we plan to fly Northwest into the center of the Arctic tomorrow morning. At the close of the service we dedicated a baby to the Lord.

February 19th. - Sunday. It must be very cold at 7:45 AM as the bedroom window has a heavy coating of ice on it. At 11:30 AM we board the 747 turbo jet plane and by 12:05, we're flying at 16,000 feet in a clear cold day northwest into the Central Arctic. I can see the ground below but everything if frozen solid and is all white.

Because we lose two hours in time from Igloolik, it's 11:10 AM and we are in a Catholic Church in Pelly Bay. This is the only church here. At 5 PM I have completed a round of visiting and witnessing the saving Grace of Jesus Christ. Also Udjualuk has been visiting.

February 20th. - 6:30 AM at Pelly Bay. I have a precious time of prayer and reading the Word. I am anxious to get out and visit again but the Inuit people do not get up until 8:30 or even 9:00, so I will just have to wait with patience. I understand that Pelly Bay is 100% Catholic. About 8:10 AM two young Inuit men came over to see me. We discussed spiritual things and both of them prayed the sinner's prayer to accept Jesus Christ as their personal Saviour. All day long Udjualuk and I visited homes and talked to many about the Lord. We've made good contacts for future work.

February 21st. - Thank God for another new day in which to glorify the Lord's name. At 8:20 AM we discover there is no water in this place because the truck broke down yesterday and it is hard to say when it will be repaired.. At 8:45 we see through our window four caribou walking past the village on the ice. It is very cold and someone said it went down to sixty degrees below zero last night. We hurried to the airport and by 10:55 we were flying at 16,000 feet on a 748 plane which is half cargo and half passengers. At 12.00 noon, we landed at Spence Bay, which is Northwest from Pelly Bay. Leaving the airport we saw more caribou on the side of the road. They called us to a table to eat partly frozen Arctic Char fish on the table. Udjualuk dug right in to eat. I wondered what they had for me. Then they brought me some spaghetti which I liked very much better. I noticed a price tag on a loaf of bread on the table says $3.57. Shortly after four we visited a home where the thermometer outside the window registered thirty six degrees below zero. In the evening we had our service in the Anglican Church. We had a full house and at 9.20 when we gave the altar call for those who wanted to accept Jesus as their Saviour and repent of their sins at least thirty five to forty came forward for salvation.After dealing with them they returned to their seats. Then we asked who needed healing to come forward for prayer. There were about fourteen who responded. Praise the Lord for the working of the Holy Spirit in the hearts of these people. Coming back to the home where I am staying I nearly froze. It must be sixty below.

February 22nd. - 7:30 AM. I noticed some red spots on my face which were frostbitten last night, although I covered up my face as much as possible. I was out all morning visiting at the Hudson Bay Trading Post, also at the Co-Op store and the municipal office. I returned home to prepare for tonight's service. They fried some caribou meat, onions and tea. All the rest of the family had a hind quarter of raw caribou which they had for dinner. Our service tonight was in the community hall which holds many more than the Anglican Church. Quite a large crowd gathered and more came in as we sang gospel choruses, in fact about three times the number that attended last night. One Inuit gave his testimony and I finished preaching through an interpreter about 8:30 so Udjualuk could preach in Inuit. When the altar call was given, many came for prayer. We thank God for working in so many hearts.

February 23rd. - 6:45 AM. Another perfect day to glorify the Lord. It is time for prayer and reading the Word. Shortly after 10 AM I went to the school and met the principal and had a good visit with him. I also met the Doctor from Edmonton and his assistant. Then I went to the store and bought five kilograms of flour which cost $12.99, one pound of lard was $2.09, one package of hardtack biscuit was $5.99, dry soup packages at $2.11 each. Canned milk cost $1.55 each. This afternoon we visited many homes and met so many who have accepted Jesus as Saviour, and also others who were healed by the power of God. We were invited out to dinner together at noon and to another home for supper. In the home where I am staying I see a caribou stomach filled with partly digested food. They tell me it's good to eat but I'm not very hungry. The service ended about 9:50 and was the best one of all. So many hungry hearts came to the altar and accepted Jesus and several received the baptism of the Holy Spirit according to Acts 2:4.

When I arrived back at the house, one of the sons of this family and his girlfriend asked me to pray for them as they wanted to be saved. So, thank God for two more. It's another very cold night, but thank God for the warm house to stay in.

February 24th. - 7:00 AM. It must be very cold as the furnace never stops. By 4 PM a blizzard is blowing. I've been visiting all day and find that the wind cuts right in. The service and altar call which ended about 9:20 PM was another great one with many coming forward for the baptism of the Holy Spirit. There was a strong, bitterly cold wind blowing as we walked home.

February 25th. - We visited more homes again today and around noon, three adult Inuits asked us to baptize them in water before we leave. We had our regular evening service in the Anglican Church at 7:00 PM, then we gathered in one of the larger homes where we held a water baptismal service. We baptized them in the bathtub. This is the first ever baptism by water immersion here at Spence Bay. Quite a number of others hesitated and decided to wait for another time. I left them singing and praising the Lord, which will likely continue until after midnight.

February 26th. - Sunday at 6:40 AM. Had time for devotions and this afternoon I arrived at an Inuit home in Gjoa Haven which has a population of about 800 people. This is our most westerly destination.The Inuit mother is here with her six children while her husband has been away for a week hunting polar bear but is expected home tonight. We attended the seven o'clock service at the Anglican Church and Pastor Paul Williams asked Udjualuk and I to speak briefly. He also asked that we conduct services in his church from Monday to Thursday night. The polar bear hunter, Jacob Atkichok, returned home about 10:00 PM.

February 27th. - After prayer and Bible reading I visited many people, witnessing for Jesus. I took time also to prepare for tonight's service. Many came forward to receive Jesus as Saviour when I gave the altar call. The people are really hungry for God and reality. One thirty year old man came to see me after the service. He was the one who accepted the Lord in last night's service, and he is so happy.

February 28th. - Got up about 6:35 AM, had a wonderful time of devotions, reading, prayer and worship; calling upon God to be merciful to these people here at Gjoa Haven and in all Arctic settlements. A visitor came and invited me to dinner. After enjoying a good caribou dinner, I returned to my cabin in a biting storm, with an Arctic wind blowing. I later visited a few people. Amundsen, the great Arctic explorer lived here at Gjoa Haven, spending two years here between 1903 and 1905. In fact, he named the place after his ship, The Gjoa. He did much scientific work here and located the North magnetic pole, and found the Northwest Passage. Udjualuk preached tonight to a good crowd and three responded to the altar call. It was a good service. At 10 PM, the same new convert who visited me last night came again tonight. We had a good time of reading the Scriptures and prayer together.

March 1st., 1989 - I had a precious time of waiting on the Lord until after 11:00 AM., then I went out visiting. Udjualuk, who stays in another Inuit home, received another call to go to a certain house to pray for a demon possessed man. He came to get me, but I had already left. He could not find me so he decided to go alone to this man's home. This man had been sick for about two years, and gradually got worse. For the past eight months he had been confined to his house. He couldn't work or hunt and could not go outdoors at all. Udjualuk, through the mighty name of Jesus, cast the demon out. Now he is free. In fact, both he and Udjualuk came to see me in the house where I was visiting. This is the first time in eight months that he had been outside, but now he is delivered, so we had a time of rejoicing, prayer, and study of the Word together. Praise the Lord!

Tonight was the largest crowd yet. Sixteen came forward for salvation. Then, while the closing hymn was being sung, another fine twenty six year old man came forward, knelt at the altar, and received Jesus as his Saviour.

March 2nd. - 6:45 AM. *This is the day the Lord hath made, I will be glad and rejoice in it,* even though there is a strong wind blowing, which means it is extra cold with the wind chill factor which makes it even worse. By two PM I returned to my cabin, the wind was bitterly cold making it around sixty degrees below zero with the wind chill factor. The ceiling and visibility was very poor. There was a good service tonight and many came forward for prayer for healing, and at least one man came for salvation. Then, that young man, who was the last to go forward last night, came with me to my cabin and we had a good time of fellowship, scripture reading and prayer together. He is so happy in the Lord.

March 3rd. - The wind howled all night. I expect the airplane to come today to fly us back to Frobisher Bay. This kind of weather is not good for flying. About 9:30 AM, Jacob, one of the catechists of the Anglican Church came to check if I was frozen or not. He told me it is very cold and strong winds are blowing, so if an Eskimo says it's cold, you can imagine how cold it is. The man at the airport reported that with the wind chill factor, it was more than eighty degrees below zero.

By 11:20 PM we were at Frobisher Bay where it is not near as cold as the Central Arctic. Thank God for a safe trip. Udjualuk told me that just before we left Gjoa Haven, the father of the family he stayed with asked him to baptize him in water. This Udjualuk did in the bathtub. As far as I know, this is the first person to be baptized by immersion in Gjoa Haven.

March 4th. - It's been a beautiful day at Frobisher Bay, which I believe is about 180 miles south of the Arctic Circle. It's about twenty five degrees below zero with no wind. We had a good breakfast at the parsonage of the church we built here in 1987. Tonight there was a good prayer time before the service which ended about 9:40 PM. It was an excellent service with a great time of worshipping and praising the Lord. The Christians here had been praying for us on our trip, so we were able to tell how God had answered their prayers, and many souls were saved. We then had a good study of the Word together.

March 5th. - Sunday. Last night before the service, one of the Eskimo men asked me to come to his home for dinner today. He lives at Apek, which is a few miles from Frobisher Bay, the original village before Frobisher Bay was built. There was a prayer time before the 11 AM service which God blessed with a fair attendance, including a few who had never attended before. There was a good response to the altar call with some weeping their way to Calvary's Cross. The young man of the family I had dinner with, is almost finished his law course and will soon be the first Inuit lawyer, as far as I know.

We had the largest crowd yet in the evening service. My interpreter sang a special number. I performed her wedding two years ago in this church. There were special blessings from the Lord during the service and many rejoiced in the Lord. I was the only white person among the Eskimos, but they thanked the Lord over and over again that we had come to minister to them and teach them the Word.

A number came to the parsonage where I was staying as they had questions to ask and I was able to show them what the Word of God said and they were satisfied.

March 6th. - I phoned the weather station this morning and was told the wind chill factor is ninety three degrees below zero.

Some of the questions asked last night were regarding marriage. In quite a number of cases, white young men enticed beautiful Inuit women to come and live with them. Soon one or two babies were born. Then, she would be invited, or wander into a gospel service, and accept Jesus as her Saviour. And now, she wanted to know what to do.

In one case, she told the white man who she was living with that she could no longer live this way, and asked him to marry her so that they could continue living as a family. He put her off saying, "Perhaps later". She refused his answer and took her children and separated. Now, a court case is pending regarding the custody of the children. She is an Inuit school teacher here.

In another case, a man agreed to get married. In fact, I performed the marriage here in this church, as well as other marriages over the years.

Still another case is pending. She has offered to marry him, but as yet he has not fully consented. She doesn't know what to do.

In last night's service, a lady came from the village on the West side of Hudson Bay. She was taking a computer course, and has problems at home and appreciated advice with Scripture backing.

It's a continuing story of life's entanglements, but Jesus is the answer. I thank God and our supporters for prayers and financial support which made this trip possible.

March 30th. - Back in Florida where we packed things in our motor home. Left Cape Coral at noon today and headed north.

April 17th., 1989 - We crossed the border at Lewiston, N.Y. after some good meetings in various churches along the way.

St. Luke 10:2-3 "Therefore said He unto them, The harvest truly is great, but the labourers are few: pray ye therefore the Lord of the harvest, that He would send forth labourers into His harvest. Go your ways: behold, I send you forth as lambs among wolves."

Cuba Trip

July 23rd., 1989 - Sunday. We were up by 6 AM. We packed two suitcases and one carry-on bag with 40 Spanish Bibles and 37 New Testaments plus Sunday School literature, clothing and fabric materials. Donald Simpson picked me up at 9:15. We drove to the Eaton Centre here in Kitchener where we met Les White who had arrived from England to make this trip to Cuba with me. He also had a good supply of Bibles in Spanish as well as cassette tapes and videos to leave in Cuba. Don drove us to the Delta Inn in Mississauga where we met Bruce who briefed us on what to expect in Cuba.

Bruce then drove us to the Toronto Airport - after a precious time of prayer for our trip. We arrived at the airport about 12:45 and took our place in the long line of passengers going to Cuba for holidays. Our suitcases and hand bags were heavy.

We had our passports and all necessary papers in order and at last we cleared Canadian Customs by 1:30 PM.

We were to board the Cuban plane by 2:30 PM., but we were told the flight was delayed until 3:30 PM. By 3:45 we had boarded the plane, which was built in Russia. I believe it compared with the 727 built in the States. By 4:10 we started to move back from the terminal and we took off at 4:30 PM. At 5:30 we were served a soft drink and cookie, others preferred beer. By 6:30, we had finished a lovely dinner of roast beef and rice, etc. At 7:10 I was up front with the Captain, Co-pilot, engineer and navigator - all Spanish. I understood them to say that after taking off from Toronto Airport, we had to stay over Canadian Territory until we were 200 miles out over the Atlantic Ocean before we turned south.

At 8:00 PM, we landed in Cuba at Varedero which is a popular holiday resort and many passengers disembarked. We took off again at 9 PM. and landed at Havana Airport at 9:35 PM. Three other planes had landed just before us. One from West Germany, one from East Germany and the other from Czechoslovakia. So the airport terminal was packed full of passengers trying to clear Cuban Customs. We were at the end of the crowd, but at last we had our passports stamped and cleared this first set of customs. Then to claim our heavy baggage, we had to show our passports to other customs officers. Another long wait before the suitcases came through. I was praying hard and by this time it was nearing midnight and all the other passengers had gone through the final customs. Many Cubans had entered this part of the terminal so I had to push and squeeze through the crowd. I could see the last Customs Officer was so tired and weary. As I neared the officer, I prayed again, "Lord help me". The officer called out "passport". I showed it to him for the third time and he said "okay". I could hardly believe my ears, but I grabbed the heavy suitcases and got past the officer and out of the airport terminal to a waiting bus. Praise the Lord! I could hardly believe it. It was a forty five minute trip to our hotel which made it about 1:30 in the morning when we arrived - dead tired.

Cuba was preparing for the great 30th anniversary celebration of the Revolution when Fidel Castro had overthrown the government on July 26th., 1959. It was a six year war which started in 1953. I understood the average wage here is $270.00 per month. There are no jobs for the people. Education is free - up to and including university and health and hospitalization is also free.

No outside preachers are allowed to preach in the churches or elsewhere. If they did, severe action could be taken against that Pastor and Church.

July 24th. We were up at 7:30 AM. Had a good breakfast and attended a tourist information meeting in the forenoon. I enjoyed a good half hour swim in the afternoon in the Atlantic Ocean and then rented a car for at least two days to accomplish what we came to do. We studied a map of Cuba and arranged our itinerary for contacts. Had a good time of fellowship with a Christian couple from El Salvador, now living in Toronto. We made arrangements with the hotel for a 6:30 AM. breakfast as we wanted to get an early start.

July 25th. - After our early breakfast, we loaded our rented car with the heavy suitcases and drove off into Havana, which has a population of two million. Cuba has ten million people. With the few Spanish street signs we found it difficult to find our way and it seemed we were driving in circles. At last, we found the street we were looking for and following it in the right direction, we soon found the Pentecostal Church. Although it was still quite early, we found quite a few people praying, including the Pastor and his staff. They were kneeling on the hard floor in intercessory prayer. A black lady, probably in her early forties, had been saved just a week before from a life of witchcraft and voodooism. She was on fire for the Lord. Speaking good English, she became our interpreter. We asked if they needed Bibles. "Oh yes," they said, "we need many Bibles." So we returned to our car and got a good supply of Bibles and New Testaments. Our interpreter received her first Bible in all her life.

We had a nice time sharing together and a precious time of prayer. The Pastor has a 1977 Nissan car which he uses in the ministry, but now its clutch is finished and he asked if we could get a new clutch for him as he was unable to get one in Havana.

By 10:45, we were on our way to the next assignment - made much easier as our interpreter guided us. We soon found the Baptist Church but it was locked and no one seemed to know where the Pastor had gone. We drove to the largest hotel where a store for tourists was located. The Cubans were not allowed to go into this store. My English friend, Les White purchased a few items and then we returned to the Baptist

Church hoping to find the Pastor and leave some Bibles, but it was still locked.

We located our next assignment by 12:50. It was a free church and the Pastor and quite a few of the staff and members were working, duplicating tapes, keeping records and general office work. This pastor was a "live wire" for God and travelled all over Cuba, visiting his out stations, and God blessed with many souls saved. Just in the last year I believe the total number of believers was over 2300, praise the Lord! The Pastor and his wife are a young couple with three small children. The wife prepared us lunch and when we asked them if they needed Bibles, the Pastor replied. "Oh yes, we need many Bibles for all these new converts."

We brought in a good supply of Bibles, New Testaments, Sunday School materials and clothing which my wife had packed up.They were overjoyed to get all this. He travelled a great deal and he told us his car was broken down and he needed another second hand car which would cost about $5000. American dollars. All food is in short supply and they even have to wait for days to get a loaf of bread, milk or eggs. On our way I asked the interpreter what the large crowds were doing. She told me they were waiting in line to get some bread and some had come six hours before to wait in line. Again, we had a precious time of fellowship, prayer and sharing with them. It was getting late in the afternoon and my stomach was beginning to act up as we took our interpreter back to her place.

The Pastor we first met had mentioned that he had to preach in a church many kilometres south-east of Havana in another town. Checking our records, we found out it was our next assignment for Bible delivery, so we took the Pastor and his wife with us. They knew the route which saved us a bit of time. When we arrived at 6 PM., the church was filled with people singing and praising the Lord. Again, we had a lovely time of sharing and prayer. What about Bibles? Yes, they needed as many as we could leave with them. They were so delighted and thankful and praised the Lord for His goodness. One of the members who could speak some English, drew us a map to take a short-cut to our hotel. My stomach was getting worse and the extreme heat was intolerable. I had not eaten since yesterday noon and I didn't even dare take a drink of water or juice. I was so glad to get back to our hotel room and near a toilet.

July 26th. - We got moving early again and my stomach is still sick. I did not eat anything last night or this morning and we had to keep going. At last, about noon we found the town which was our next assignment. We had a Pastors name but no address and when we tried to inquire if anyone knew the Pastor, it was in vain so we drove further and continued asking. At last one man motioned to wait and he ran off and brought another man, a school teacher who spoke English. He was Catholic and knew the Pastor and where he lived. We drove up one street and down another, around a corner to where he said it was. This was a very poor part of town and at last we found a member of the church who told us the Pastor was away to a Baptist Camp but they didn't know where the Camp was. After much searching and perseverance, we found a Baptist Church with a Pastor who gave us directions. We were to travel about sixteen kilometres in one direction, turn left and travel another three or four kilometres, take another sharp left at a gas station and keep going for many kilometres until we saw the sign for the Baptist Camp.

What a road, with huge holes all across it. In some places we had to leave the road altogether to get around the holes. We drove up a long hill and down into a valley for miles. Then we saw the sign, what a wonderful campground and many buildings. Here we found the Pastor we were looking for. He was the Administrator of the camp and many men and women were working hard cleaning up, washing, painting and doing carpentry work.

The day before they had just completed a seminar for many Bible students from all over Cuba. The next day they expected approximately four hundred boys and girls to arrive in cars and busses from all over the country. We asked if they needed Bibles. By this time we should have known better than to ask that question. We brought in all the Bibles, New Testaments and Sunday School materials we had left. They were overjoyed, delighted and so thankful to the Lord. Before we left, we asked what the greatest needs were and they all said, "prayer and more Bibles". We had a good time of fellowship, sharing and prayer and then headed back to our hotel. Our mission was accomplished successfully because of your prayer and financial support.

We took our rented car back - it cost $40.00 per day plus insurance, plus gasoline and mileage at twenty cents a kilometre. But without that car, what can we do? It was well worth every dollar spent. Every day groups of tourists were coming and leaving the hotel, groups from Russia, West Germany, East Germany, Czechoslovakia and other countries. I found those who could speak and understand some English. It was a joy to witness to these people each day. The flight crews knew English as communications around the world to Air Traffic Control Towers must be in English. Some listened carefully, others asked questions and I gave them Bible Scripture answers. What a joy to spend time with those people for whom Jesus died. Even some of the Cuban policemen and officials at the hotel heard the gospel.

While some were out sight-seeing on tours, others swimming in the ocean or pool and still others getting a sun-tan, I had the most precious time of all, in my room in intercessory prayer for the people of Cuba and all that I witnessed to, that the Holy Spirit would work in each heart, that the seed sown would germinate and grow bringing forth fruit and that God will bless each gospel Pastor and encourage their hearts.

By Thursday night, I was able to eat a little supper and drink fruit juice, I began to get well, thank the Lord. But then my partner took sick and did not eat until we arrived back in Canada on July 30th.

July 29th. - My last day at the hotel. I had many good opportunities to witness. Then about 9 PM a Christian couple and their daughter whom I presume to be about twenty years old, came to visit me. They could speak some English, especially the daughter who was in her third year at university. They didn't have a Bible and wondered if I had one for them. The only one I had was my own New Testament which I was reading, but I gave to the girl. She was so happy and the parents were overjoyed although they could not read English. We shared together, then had prayer just outside the hotel. When I opened my eyes, there was a policeman nearby watching but he didn't bother us.

July 30th. - Sunday and I was awake at 3 AM. to get packed up and ready for our trip home. In the Havana Airport I met a Russian diplomat from the Russian Embassy. He could speak some English. Naturally, he was a Communist but as I witnessed, he was interested in the good message. Who knows?

I met another university student who was in her fourth year of studies to become a doctor. She appeared interested in the gospel message. We had a long talk and as she didn't have a Bible, I promised to get one for her as I had no more.

Please pray for these Cubans and others who we contacted, that the Holy Spirit will enlighten and draw them to Jesus. Truly the harvest is great but the labourers are few.

1989 Fall Arctic Trip

August 28th., 1989 - I got up about 4:30 AM and packed most of my things in my suitcase. I had already packed Bibles, New Testaments and gospel literature in another suitcase. At six I made breakfast and Tyyne packed three lunches, one for Daniel as he works every day, one for pilot Jay who was flying in from the States in a twin engine plane and one for myself.

We had our morning devotions and a phone call from our daughter Grace in Kirkland Lake to say goodbye.

Jay arrived in his Aztec about 9:45 AM and we were airborne and heading north at 10:35. By 11:10 we were way above the clouds at 11000 feet. We had part of the lunch which my wife Tyyne prepared, a sandwich, coke and orange juice just before noon as we flew over North Bay. By 1:25 PM we were passing over Mattagami and we enjoyed the rest of the lunch. The weather was getting colder as we flew north and temperature reading was zero degrees C.

At three o'clock we descended through the clouds as we had a 3000' ceiling and we approached to land at LG2. It was cold enough that I had to put my heavy parka on over my sweater as we refuelled the plane. It took 424 litres of gas for $345.56. We checked the weather further north but it was zero, zero. So I rented a car which cost $75 per day and we drove the twenty miles to the hotel which cost $95 per night. We refuelled with forty five gallons at $7.66 per gallon.

August 29th. - At 7:00 AM the weather looked fine so we drove to the airport and shortly after 9 we were taxiing out for the take off. By 10:45 AM we had to turn around and go back to Great Whale River which we passed enroute north to Umiujaq. We got within five miles of the village under the clouds, but then the clouds lowered to below the hills, so we had no choice but to go back up on top and head south.

We were back at Great Whale at 11:10 AM. While we waited on the weather, we met one of the chief men from here. He recognized me and asked us to have a service in his home in Inukjuak and stay at his house. Around two o'clock we took off again for Umiujaq. We got so close but the fog was down to the ground so we had no choice but to climb to the top and return to Great Whale. By the time we got back, the fog had come in and we only had 200' ceiling and limited visibility. We tried three times to land before we made it.

This evening we witnessed to the local people as well as a young couple from Ottawa. Had prayer with them all.

August 30th. - At. 6:30 AM the fog was hanging low but to be prepared, we put in another thirty five gallons of gas this morning. The airport had four big plane loads to go to Umiujaq but no plane could go in. My Inuit friend, Willie, phoned me. and told me the fog was still there. The rest of the morning I spent out witnessing for the Lord.

About 2:30 we took off and were at Willie's home by 3:40. where Jay and I were to stay. The ceiling coming over was 500' all the way. We had hoped for 1000' and thanked the Lord for a safe trip.

Tonight there was a service in our church at Umiujaq.

Brother Jay followed the wonderful spirit filled singing and worship service with a powerful message on Matt. 16:13-18, "Whom do you say I am". Billy, the guitarist, who led the singing, interpreted. Then I preached on Romans 8:28 to the end of the chapter. At the close of the service, we prayed for many. The ship arrived this evening with a year's supply of gas and oil.

August 31st. - When I got up at 6:15 AM, fog covered the whole area right down to the ground. I had a good time of study and prayer for our next service.

Jay and I visited most of the morning, meeting the people including the president of the council. By lunch time the fog lifted a little.

We had a precious time of worship and praise in the evening service. Brother Jay preached first and then I preached. More people attended than last night and many came up for prayer. I thank the Lord for all His goodness.

September 1st., 1989 - At 6:35 AM the weather didn't look too bad for flying and we took off at 9:45 in a cold rain and gusty winds. It was comforting to know I had my heavy parka and the radio said it was snowing at Cape Dorset. Our windshield and wings began icing up but as soon as we got up on top it was clear and the ice began burning off although the temperature was twelve below zero.

By 11.00 AM, we were on the ground at Inukjuak thanking the Lord for a safe trip. We were treated to a good dinner of caribou meat at one of our Christian's homes. They then took us to another Christian's home for the night service. Quite a few people gathered in the home and we sang some good hymns and choruses and praised the Lord. Brother Jay preached first and after, I gave some words of appreciation for seeing so many people attend the gospel service. We prayed for some to be better Christians and others for various needs. About 10:40 the service ended and we were able to sleep tonight in this home.

September 2nd. - Early morning the clouds were not too high, but we checked the flying conditions and weather at Povungnituk by phone and decided to give it a try. Enroute we ran into some rough weather with snow flurries, and wondered if we'd have to turn back. We continued and were able to land on the very rough gravel landing strip. When we taxied to park the plane, we hit a soft spot of sand. One of the propellers hit the sand and got a little damaged so we had to go to the village and get one of the Eskimo men to help us repair the damage. Then I got a 45 gallon drum of gasoline and a hand pump and we refuelled. By 1:35 PM, we were in one of the Eskimo homes and Elizabeth, the mother was preparing

Arctic Char fish for our dinner.

The service began late in our little church in Povungnituk as most of the people were out picking blueberries and didn't return until late - but they wanted a service anyway. We had a great service and a good altar call with quite a few responding. Then we dedicated a little boy to the Lord.

September 2nd. - When we got up at 6 this morning the weather was heavy fog right down to the ground. The sun had it burned off though by shortly after 9:00 giving us a 1000' ceiling to take off in. We were able to climb through the top at 5000' where there was nice sunshine as we headed for Ivujivik. At 10:15 AM we were flying through broken clouds and we could see the ground in some places. There were patches of snow here and there and as we passed over latitude 62, our temperature was 12 degrees below zero.

The service began late in our Ivujivik church and there was a real power of God flowing as we worshipped. It was about 1:20 AM when they sang the closing hymn after we had prayed for quite a number at the altar. It is just marvellous what God is doing in these hearts. There is a real sincerity as they worship God with eyes closed and hands raised in worship.

September 3rd. - Sunday. Our evening service began tonight at 6 PM with many people giving their testimonies. After 10 PM many were still coming up for prayer in a service that lasted long. As the Lord was in our midst, much was accomplished for His glory.

September 4th. - It was foggy and low overcast at 6:30 AM. We refuelled at 9:45 AM using two drums of gas at $688.23. After checking the weather for Cape Dorset, we took off but shortly after noon we landed at Wakeham Bay as the Cape Dorset weather was not so good.

Many people were out camping and hunting today which is Labour Day. The Pastor arrived home about 10:00 PM and Jay and I had a long visit with them.and then returned to the home where we were staying. It was so cold I was glad to have my long winter underwear on, gloves on my hands and my heavy parka.

September 5th. - We awoke to heavy fog today which stayed with us all day. Tonight we gathered in our lovely church which is 64' x 30'. What a joy to hear the Inuit choruses being sung and to see the Mayor of this town play drums while his wife leads the worship. I performed their marriage three years ago. As the service continued, our Pastor played the electric organ accompanied by a guitarist. A former Mayor gave his testimony about how he was opposed to us to found a Full Gospel church here when we asked permission of the local council, but now he is saved and rejoicing in the Lord.

The largest crowd yet on this trip turned out for the service and Brother Jay preached. There were many responding to the altar call, some for salvation, others for rededication and others for healing. We thank God for a great move of the Holy Spirit.

September 6th. - This morning I checked the weather at 4:45 AM to find we had scattered fog so I went back to bed until 7:00 and the fog was worse. I made breakfast for Jay and I and then phoned the weather station at Great Whale to find this bad weather exists all across the Arctic. I was to officiate at a wedding at Ivujivik tonight and also baptize three in water but everything is now on hold until we get better weather.

At 12:30 there was still heavy fog. Air Inuit was supposed to fly in at 11 this morning but they cancelled this flight. Annie, our Pastor. wants another service tonight if we are still here. This afternoon, Jay and I visited and met people who were here so many years ago when I first visited Kangiqsujuaq. It remained foggy with a very cold rain and wind all day.

It was a wonderful service this evening with Brother Jay preaching. Lasting until about 10:00 PM, there must have been fifteen or sixteen who came up for prayer, salvation, healing or rededication. On the way back from the church, we prayed for a sick woman, and also dedicated a new home which a family had moved into two weeks ago. Before the service, I learned there will be two couples to be married tomorrow night, weather permitting. We plan to fly to Cape Dorset and pick up a young man to fly to Ivujivik so that he can marry a young girl there, God willing. Some how I believe the Lord has delayed us here for some reason as we witnessed and visited this afternoon.

September 7th. - 6:00 AM and the weather was looking better! By 7:20 we were in the plane at the airport warming up for it was zero degrees and we planned to fly direct to Cape Dorset.

By 12:30 PM we had a good flight from Kangiqsujuaq to Cape Dorset on top of the clouds, but the plane heater didn't work and both of us were so cold. The temperature at 8000' was twelve below zero. After Jay took off and climbed above the clouds, I flew the plane to Cape Dorset. We brought one young man from Cape Dorset to Ivujivik to be married tonight. Jay and I went first to one of our Christian homes for lunch. At 4:10 I had completed all the paper work for the two weddings tonight.

By 6:05 the service had started in our church in Ivujivik and Brother Jay preached the sermon as I looked forward to performing the wedding for the two couples as well as a water baptismal service. At 9:00 PM the weddings were over and we had baptized one man in water, after he gave a wonderful testimony. Another hymn was sung and then I baptized two more. By 9:30 everyone was singing again and the wonderful service ended at 10:10 PM. God's presence was so real!

September 8th. - We bought gas at 4:50 AM, and then packed up. I made breakfast and one of our brothers drove us to the airport, but heavy frost covered the plane, so we had a big job to take all the frost off.

We landed at LG2 at 11:00 AM, refuelled, checked the weather and filed the flight plan. We were ready for take off at 11:50 AM and at 2:55 PM, we were 55 miles north of Rouyn; we came through some terrific thunderstorms, lightning flashing and very heavy rains. It then became much better. We were at 8000' but the turbulence was so violent, the plane jerked up and down and then twisted sideways. So we descended to 6000' and then on down to 4000' Eventually we flew into better weather and climbed back up to 10000' The Airtransport had us on radar and called to us on the radio saying they thought for sure we had been hit by lightning. But God protected us and we give Him all the glory.

At 4:50 PM, we descended to land at the Kitchener Airport.

Chapter 11

That They Might Be Saved

Romans 10:1 "Brethren, my heart's desire and prayer to God for Israel is, that they might be saved."

March 11th., 1990. Sunday. Tyyne and I left Cape Coral, Florida this morning at 8 AM and drove to the Christian Retreat in Bradenton in time for the morning service. There was a large crowd in attendance and we met many friends including the Stockdales who invited us for dinner. We also attended the evening service at six and God moved in both services. We stayed at Miracle Manor overnight.

March 12th. - The group travelling to Israel met in the lobby, and we all drove to Tampa airport TWA counter where we checked our bags for Tel Aviv. Then we flew to JFK Airport in New York where we met the rest of our group. We boarded a 1011 TWA and took off at 8 PM and flew to Paris arriving there at approximately 3:30 AM.

March 13th. - It's Tuesday and we took off again at 4:30 AM U.S. time and landed in Tel Aviv at 9:18 AM U.S. time which is 4:18 PM local time. At 5:40 PM we toured the city of Joppa and our guide told us the history of this place, of Jonah and Peter. We arrived at the Blue Bay Hotel in Netanya, Israel, just north of Tel Aviv at 8:20 PM. We had a lovely supper of roast beef, etc.

March 14th. - Up at 6:30 and it was a beautiful day. At 10 PM we met with eight special Christian Arab pastors in the Plaza Hotel in Tiberias. It was so exciting to hear from their own lips how so many Arabs are being saved. One Arab had a contract to kill Gerald Derstine for $4,000.00. While Gerald was in Canada preaching, this Arab was lying on his bed resting, when Gerald walked into his room and talked to him about Jesus and led him to accept Jesus as his Saviour. He is now pastor of many born again Christians. Two of these pastors have been killed by Arabs hostile to Christianity.

One Arab family was very hostile. But one day, Mrs. Gerald Derstine walked into her room and talked to her and won her to Jesus. This just happened a few days before and now the whole family is saved and many others who had listened to the gospel message. Mrs. Derstine however, was at the Christian Retreat in Florida when this happened. How can you explain this miracle?

The pastors we were meeting emphasized how willing they

were to lay down their lives for Jesus' sake. Some of these men were from the Golan Heights near the Syrian border, and now many Syrian Arabs are believers. One Arab Israeli mayor of a town plans to go to Bible School at Christian Retreat this summer and a few other men in government offices also plan to go to Bible School. God is doing a great miracle in Israel and the Christian Arabs are pleading for our prayers.

March 15th. At 3:15 PM, we were in the home of the Druze woman who had this experience of Beulah, Mrs. Gerald Derstine, coming into her room and in pure Arabic language, witnessing to her and winning her to Jesus. Now was the first time she met Beulah in person since her experience, and she recognized her as the same person. The house was full of people. She is a school teacher and she taught the Moslem religion but now she has turned totally around and teaches the Bible to the children. The whole village is stirred tremendously.

At 3:50 PM more people came in and were so excited to tell what the Lord was doing. So many of these Arabs had accepted Jesus as their Saviour. Among them is the man who accepted the contract to kill Gerald Derstine and now he too has accepted Jesus as Saviour and is our brother in Jesus.

At 4:20 PM we were in another beautiful Arab home. It was a mansion and the owner is a believer in Jesus Christ. He has a large business supplying fruits and vegetables to hotels and restaurants and many men work for him. I understand there were more than 1500 Arabs saved and it's growing rapidly. One Arab man spoke and was so happy that we came to visit and encourage them. By 5:40 PM we were in another Arab village, 9 kilometres from where we were visiting. This was the home of a pastor who was saved recently and now about thirty others have been saved and the Holy Spirit is moving upon many more hearts.We were told at 6:10 PM, by one of the Arab brothers that they were under much persecution and meet after midnight to worship the Lord. They taught and studied the Bible together and prayed and sought the Lord. So, this was another church just started.

March 16th. - Tiberias and up at 5 AM. We drove to the Jordan River for a water baptismal service for a number of Arab new Christians. Each gave a wonderful testimony, interpreted by an Arab pastor. What a wonderful time of praise and rejoicing as each one was baptized. Then we drove south along the Jordan River to Jericho and south to Elat on the Red Sea. We followed the coast of the Dead Sea where we saw large hills of salt.

March 17th. - Was up at 3.45 at Elat on the Red Sea. At 6:40 we were at the Egyptian border where we had to fill in forms, have our passports stamped and pay our entrance fee.

Then we were on our way shortly with our Egyptian driver, Egyptian guide and also an Israeli guide. I had a wonderful opportunity to witness to the lady in charge of the hotel in Elat and one Jewish man. I mentioned how many Arabs had accepted Jesus as Saviour in Upper Galilee and they said, "We know about it."

At 12 noon we were at Sinai, 4500' high - they say where Moses came fleeing from Egypt, where he met Jethro. A well is here where Moses helped to water the sheep and goats of Jethro. Moses spent 40 years with Jethro, then God sent him to Egypt. We saw the monastery built in the 6th Century where 40 Greek Orthodox monks look after it.

March 19th. - Monday. In Jerusalem yesterday on our way here we stopped at the place where David killed Goliath. Today we visited the Wailing wall and temple site. As we left the Mount of Olives, two young Arab men threw stones at our bus breaking the windshield and one side window. We had dinner at a Christian Arab home, and a few other Arab brothers came. One of these Arab men told us that he and five other Arabs took an oath to kill one of the Arabs who had become a Christian. They drove to this man's home and five of them stayed in the car while their leader, armed with knives, went in to kill this man. When he opened the door to rush in, this Christian Arab was reading God's Word aloud to other Arabs who had gathered in for a meeting. The Word of God arrested this killer and he returned to the car and commanded the driver to return to Jerusalem. Now that same killer and three other Arabs are born again Christians. But two other Christian Arab leaders have been killed.

One of these other Arab men started to build a large two story concrete building for a school for Moslem children. He was one of the leaders of the Moslems in that area. The Christians were praying for him and the Holy Spirit worked in his heart and he got in touch with the Christian Arabs and surrendered to the Lord. Now he has turned this building over to Gospel Crusade to be used for a school for Christian Arab children. He has already spent approximately $250,000.00 in building it, but another $150,000.00 is needed to complete it.

March 20th. - We were in the Upper Room at 10:40 AM praising and worshipping the Lord. We read the scripture in Acts 2 that the promise of the Spirit is for every believer. A message in tongues and the interpretation was given. At 12:15 PM we gathered in the International Christian Embassy for a service. Many of our group had come to Israel for the first time. At 4:05 PM we were in the Garden Tomb and Golgatha area where a service was in progress for some time ending with a communion service. About 4:45 PM I read the resurrection story in Luke and a number of our group gave witness to their experience in the Lord. Then one of the Arab pastors, a former Moslem, testified to his experience in being born again. He was greatly encouraged that he could fellowship with us. Gerald Derstine came to Jerusalem in '88 and held a three week school of Ministry and this man attended, although he was not saved and still a Moslem. But his heart was longing for reality. Gerald just mentioned that thirteen of these students were Moslems but hungry for God. Before the Bible Study ended, all thirteen of these Moslems accepted Jesus as their personal Saviour and this man was one of them. The wonderful service of prayer, praise and worship and partaking of communion ended at 5:15 PM. At 11:05 PM we concluded a very lengthy meeting in the conference room of our hotel with six Arab leaders plus a seeking Moslem man. Their main need is for prayer, then for thousands of Bibles in Arab languages, also for help to furnish two school buildings and one more church. These Arab men are real genuine leaders, soul winners in the truest sense.

March 21st. - Visited Masada. I had a good opportunity to witness to two Israeli soldiers. We talked of the unrest and tension in Israel and the hatred of the Arabs. I was able to tell them that many Arabs have now accepted Jesus as their personal Saviour and that last night we heard Arab leaders testify that they love the Jews in Israel and they want total peace. I was also able to tell these Israeli soldiers that there is only one way to have peace and that is to accept the Prince of Peace, Jesus the Messiah. They asked many questions and I told them the answers from the Word. I advised them to get the New Testament and to read and do what it says. I do believe that seed was sown in their hearts that will bring forth fruit unto eternal life.

March 23rd. - In Jerusalem at 3:30 AM, we had a good meeting with Mohammed, an Arab Christian who teaches 22 Arabs in a village nearby. He came to see us here in the hotel and asked us to pray for him, to be able to buy the building he is renting as the owner wants to sell it as soon as possible. We had a wonderful time of fellowship and prayer in our room in the hotel as our group gathered in. God has been really blessing in Israel and many are being saved, but the old devil is also working against God's people. Please pray for these people.

8:45 AM. We came to the airport at 5:30 AM and the terminal was packed with travellers so it took a long time to clear customs and security and then to load all those passengers. I believe every seat was filled. In the first thirty minutes that I had been in my seat, I had a good opportunity to talk to a young Jewish man next to me that Jesus is the Messiah. He asked me many questions which he said he had thought about for a long time but had not an opportunity to talk to any one about these questions before. The Captain informed us the flight would be 11 hours and 35 minutes to New York. We took off from Tel Aviv at 9:02 AM and landed in New York at 8:28 PM., local time 1:28 PM.

April 2nd. 1990 - We left Cape Coral, Florida and began our trip north.

Isaiah 43:6 "I will say to the north, Give up; and to the south, Keep not back: bring my sons from far, and my daughters from the ends of the earth."

May 14th. 1990 - Was up at 6 AM. Five degrees celsus and a lovely morning. Jay flew in at 9.20 AM and 30 minutes later we refuelled, loaded the plane and were ready to fly. We landed at North Bay at 11:25 AM. Our compass was acting up so we had to get it fixed. I flew the plane all the way here. By 12:40 the compass was fine and we were ready to take off. At 3:35 PM we are in white wonderland landing at L.G. 2 about 50 miles inland from the north end of James Bay. The ground is covered with snow and the lake is frozen over. At 4:10 we re-fuelled and took off. We took a little over 100 U.S.. gallons of fuel and then flew over to Fort Chimo. Jay Byers took off and landed and I flew VFR although we came through rain and snow showers for about 100 miles. At 6:45 Jay took over the controls as we descended and landed at Fort Chimo. It's real winter here and we are on the south edge of the Arctic. Do they charge here, after paying a huge price for fuel, it was $24.75 landing fees and $40.00 for after hours refuelling. We took off again at 7:35 PM as we wanted to reach Kangiqsujuaq (Wakeham Bay) if possible. At 7:50 we were up in the fog and climbed to 8000'. Jay was doing all the flying now. We ate the lunch which Tyyne made for each of us and it was very good. Temperature had dropped to ten below zero. At 9:35 PM we were descending to land at Kangiqsujuaq and we flew over the village hoping to get someone to come and get us. 10:30 PM. The pastor and Udjualuk and a few from the church came to get us. It was awfully cold and much snow, real winter as the snow has not begun to melt yet. Three of us were in one of the church members lovely homes.

May 15th. - Although it was time to get up at 7:30 AM, we were very tired for yesterday was a hard day. We were in the plane at 10:45 AM, warming up the engine for take off. At 11:00 AM we were at 7000' and it was 10 below zero as we flew north across the Hudson Strait. At 11:45 we descended to land at Frobisher Bay. The evening service in our church here at Frobisher Bay was well underway by 7:50 PM and although not on a regular service night, a few Inuits gathered in. The Holy presence of God was in this place in our worship and praise. Jay and Wilfred Remus shared and I brought the message from God's Word about God's covenant with His people. It was a great service.

May 16th. - At 7:30 AM it was four degrees below zero and snowing hard. The weather cleared enough for take-off and at 11:50 AM we were in the plane after paying $7.27 per American gallon in advance for 220 gallons of gas further north. 40 minutes later we were at 8000', just near the top of the cloud cover and the temperature was fifteen below zero. Ten minutes later we levelled off at 9500' on top where it was twenty two degrees below zero. The jagged peaks below us began to appear at 1:40 PM and the glaciers were fantastic. We had to go up to 10,000' to clear the peaks and by 1:55 PM we were descending to land at Broughton Island. At 6:45 PM we were in the lovely church here in Broughton Island as the people were gathering in and we expected a wonderful time in the presence of the Lord. We'd already had a wonderful time of prayer before the service began. It was still continuing at 8:45 PM with each of us sharing, first Jay Byers, the pilot preached. Thank God for a good altar service and time of praise and worship and by 9:45 PM we are back to our sleeping quarters many miles north of the Arctic Circle.

May 17th. - It's daylight night and day here. The Pastor and people asked us to stay over to have another service tonight. We were out all morning meeting people and witnessing. We went to the Hudson Bay store and bought groceries, everything was very expensive. By 6:45 PM people were gathering in the church. The Mayor of Broughton Island plays the keyboard and many influential people come from this assembly.By 7:40 PM we'd had a precious time of praise and worship. I'd asked Udjualuk to preach but the other three of us would share a few words so I was the first to speak and chose Heb. 11:6, that *"God is a rewarder to those that diligently seek him."* Brother Will Remus followed me and by 8:20, Brother Jay gave his testimony and shared with us. Then the congregation sang an invitation chorus and one girl, about twenty years old ran up to the altar and with strong crying and tears and wept her way though to God at the mercy seat after we prayed for her. Then a young married woman came forward, again with strong crying and tears. She too touched Jesus. Then Udjualuk began to preach a message from Joshua 24:15. At 9:05 PM about a dozen came forward at the altar call again with many tears flowing and God touched many hearts and a great work was done by the Holy Spirit.

May 18th. - Fourteen degrees below zero at 6:40 AM. This is considered really mild for up here. At 10:55 it was eleven below zero. We loaded everything in the plane and warmed up the engines. The fog was right down to the ground in places while other areas were clear. We took off and climbed up on top enroute to Pond Inlet, 425 Knots away which is 495 miles. We descended to land at Pond Inlet at 4:50 PM. At 5:55 PM we were all in different homes but at 6:10 PM they moved me into the same home as Wilf Remus. It was nice that the two of us were together.

We'd had quite a day. We left Broughton Island at 11:00 AM and climbed up over the fog. Jay tried to get the heater working but it refused. He worked hard on it for half an hour and we descended to keep flying north and land at Clyde River to fix it. At 1:30 PM we were all very cold - nearly frozen. We found Clyde River and descended from 10500' to 5000'. Then suddenly, the heater came alive and heated the cabin quickly, so instead of landing, we decided to continue on north to Pond Inlet. About 20 minutes later, the heater quit and we returned and landed at Clyde River. Jay was able to fix it and we all got somewhat thawed in the airport terminal. It was 3:15 when we left Clyde River for Pond Inlet. The flight was so nice and warm when everything was working properly.

We met some fine people here and the lady of the home cooked some caribou for our supper. By 7:55, quite a few people had gathered in this home for a service. At 9.00 quite a few Inuit were here and appeared hungry for the Word. Each one of us shared a message. I spoke on 1st John 5:11-13. Then Jay spoke. The lady of this home was our interpreter and did a good job. Brother Wilf Remus spoke on Gal. 5:22, 23. Udjualuk did the main preaching beginning about 9:20 and he spoke on Acts 2:17-18. Then we opened the meeting for questions and quite a few inquired of the Baptism of the Holy Spirit. I showed them from the scripture that the promise is for every believer. A wonderful time of prayer and praise followed and God touched many hearts.

May 19th. - At 7:30 AM it was time to get up and by 8:10 I had a good bath and went to see what I could find for breakfast. We'd been out to the airport to check the plane by 10:40 AM and the weather was not good, snowing and blowing very badly. We returned to where Wilf and I were staying as they wanted another service tonight. At 8:30 PM we were in the Anglican church parish hall, having arrived before 8 for the service to which many people came. Jay, Wilf and I spoke for a few minutes and Udjualuk preached the gospel message which ended with an altar call about 10:05. Many came forward for prayer and at 10:50 PM we were asked to visit a home to pray for a sick man. After a time of prayer with him, he accepted Jesus as Saviour. We were back in our room about 11:35 PM.

May 20th. - Sunday and the storm has abated. At 7:40 AM it is a beautiful sunny day. Of course, up here it's daylight and sunlight night and day. I went downstairs to see what I could find for breakfast while Wilf was washing.We attended the 11:30 morning service at the Anglican church. By 7:10 PM we were back at the Anglican church for the evening service and a very large crowd came as we trusted the Lord for His bless- ing. By 7:30 Udjualuk had spoken before he played and sang a special solo. I preached the Good News of the Gospel and gave the altar call by 9:30 with many coming to receive Jesus, while others came to be better Christians and some for heal- ing. Udjualuk closed in prayer.

May 21st. - It was 6:45 AM and I was anxious to get going. We had to pump two drums of gas in the plane at $400.00 per drum. At 11:25 we had loaded everything and were warming up the engines for take-off to Nanisivik and Arctic Bay. Arrived in Nanisivik at 1:40 PM. We passed over here quite some time ago and we were advised that this airport was closed with zero zero weather, so we decided to fly on to Resolute Bay. The winds were very strong and after flying for some time, we were advised that the Resolute Bay weather was closing in. So we turned to fly back to Pond Inlet and even there the weather was closing. Jay looked over the left side of the plane and there was a hole in the clouds and he saw some buildings which we recognized as Nanisivik, so we descended to 4000' and followed the road out to the airport. Blowing snow obscured visibility but Jay landed with an ex- tremely strong cross wind. Thank God the airport terminal was open and it was warm there.

At 2:40 PM we used the pay phone to call Arctic Bay, about 20 miles from here. They said the blizzard was so bad that the road was closed and must be opened with the snow plow. That could take quite a few hours, so we brought food from the plane and made ourselves quite comfortable until they could come and get us. By 3:55 PM, the wind was between 30 and 35 miles an hour. We put the wing covers and engine tents on and oh what a job! The temperature was thirty below just before we landed.

The Big snow plow trucks broke a road through 6' and 8' drifts with two trucks behind and rescued us from the airport at 5:30 PM. This was six or seven miles away and they brought us to Nanisivik mine settlement. Here we were inside a home, but the storm was terrific as we could not see a car length ahead of us in places. The storm worsened as the evening continued however we were able to have a Bible

Study and prayer with people of this home.

May 22nd. - Although the blizzard raged hard all night long it seemed at 6:50 AM that it was beginning to let up. We all slept in our sleeping bags and had a good rest.Eventually a snow plow pushed a path through snow drifts up to 8' high to Arctic Bay, about twenty miles from Nanisivik and then a 3/4 ton truck came about 5.00 PM and brought us to Pastor Charles home in Arctic Bay. The service was scheduled for 7:00 PM and I noticed at 7:10 that although quite a few had arrived, still even more were coming. There was a real spirit of worship and praise as we sang choruses and by 8:45, the three of us had shared a short message and Udjualuk started preaching. The altar call was about 9:30 PM and many came forward for prayer for salvation, for healing and to become stronger Christians.

May 23rd. - We were out all morning visiting at the Hudson Bay Company and the only other store in the community and we inspected the very short airstrip which is o.k. for a twin engine plane but not for an Aztec. Had Arctic char for dinner and about 1:45 PM I went to the church where I could pray and intercede for the evening service, that precious souls would be saved and many hearts touched. By 3:00 the storm was getting worse. We had planned to fly to Resolute Bay, re-fuel and then fly to Grise Fiord tomorrow, but decided to wait and see what the weather was like in the morning.

I was in the church and ready for the service at 6:50 PM when a phone call came from Nanisivik telling me the roads are all blocked with snow drifts and the Eskimos who work at the mine but live in Arctic Bay can not come home tonight because the roads are impassable. They had to spend the night in Nanisivik. At 7:35 PM there was a bigger crowd that last night and could they ever sing! At 8:30 I finished preaching on Col. 1:9-14 and there was a real spirit of conviction here. Then Udjualuk spoke on John 10:9, 10. There was another wonderful altar service and more adults came forward and accepted Jesus as Saviour. Others came forward for prayer to become better Christians and workers for the Lord. Outside the storm was still raging.

May 24th. - At 7:00 AM it was a beautiful sunny day, in fact the sun shines day and night here all summer, but we couldn't get to the airport twenty miles away until the road was plowed. It must have been very cold outside because the furnace was going most of the time. The road was supposed to be open by 9 AM, so we left Arctic Bay about 10:35 to drive to the airport. We managed to get eight miles out, getting stuck a few times and then we came upon a huge snowdrift. We turned around and went back to the Pastor's home. Finally the plow came through and we drove to the airport, took off the wing and engine covers, put more oil in both engines and at 12:35 PM we started and were warming them up for take-off. At 2:10 PM we began our descent to land at Resolute Bay fifteen miles away, down from 10500' to 3000'. At 3 .00 PM, after taking on 605 litres of fuel we began warming up to fly to Griese Fiord. One hour and thirty five minutes later we were just eight miles from Griese Fiord.

Udjualuk and I stayed in one home, Wilf in another and Jay in another. I went over to see the Anglican minister. They have only one Sunday service but he said for us to use his church for a meeting at 8 PM. Griese Fiord is the closest Eskimo village to the North Pole. It's on Ellesmere Island.

8:10 PM the service had started and a few people had arrived. The Anglican pastor opened in prayer and Udjualuk played his accordion and led in the singing. Then the gospel was preached once again in Grise Fiord. No one responded to the altar call but at least the Holy Spirit will bring it back for God's Word will not return void. This was the first service we held on this trip when no one came forward for prayer. Although the weather was clear all day and even warm when we went to church, after service it was snowing hard.

May 25th. - A lovely day and at 9:10 AM it was ten degrees below zero. We removed the wing and engine covers and got the engines started and warming up. As the regular compass is no good up here, we had to use electronic instruments to fly at all or by vision. We were sitting at the end of the runway at 10:30 AM ready for take off. Jay checked the heater and it didn't work so we couldn't take off until we got it working as temperatures at 10000' are twenty to thirty degrees below zero, so Jay worked on the heater. At 12:45 PM we landed at Resolute Bay, half frozen. By 2:15 PM the heater was working and we'd refuelled and were preparing to take off for Igloolik. Fifteen minutes later we were at 7000' into the overcast where there was some icing but it didn't get too bad and the heater worked so we were comfortable. We landed at Igloolik about 4:20 and at 6:15 PM we were all eating supper at Pastor Peter Awa's home. Lots of good Arctic char, mashed potatoes, corn, etc., etc.

At 7:15 PM we were in our lovely Full Gospel Church in Igloolik. Pastor Peter opened in prayer and Udjualuk played his accordion. Quite a few people were here praising the Lord and Elizabeth, the Pastor's wife, led the singing and played her tambourine. 10:45 PM saw the end of another great service and many came forward for prayer when the altar call was given. We thank God for the moving of the Holy Spirit upon these precious people.

May 26th. - It's a lovely sunny day at 7:50 AM but quite cool. The Pastor and his wife and some of the family went camping and fishing last night after the service and will not return until tonight. The four of us were up so I decided to see what I could find for breakfast. At 11:15 AM we had refuelled and the engines were warming up for take-off to Cape Dorset. Thirty minutes later, the heater stopped working but we had no choice but to keep flying with no cabin heat so we climb up to 6000' and flew direct to Cape Dorset.

At 7:40 PM we were in our lovely Full Gospel Church in Cape Dorset which we built in 1979. The singing and praising was wonderful as we worshipped the Lord. The wonderful service ended about 10:10 and I believe there were eight or nine who came forward for prayer. God blessed in a wonderful way.

May 27th. - Sunday and by 11:10 AM we had gathered in the church and were praising the Lord and thanking Him for His blessings. Udjualuk led the singing and played his accordion, while the pastor and another brother played guitars and still another brother played drums. Before leaving the pastor's home to come to church they mentioned they would have goose for dinner and we were invited. At 12:10 PM Jay was preaching on Matt. 16:13-18, and the pastor interpreted. Another great service ended about 12:50 and then everyone shook hands in greeting and we returned to the pastor's home for a goose dinner.

7:30 PM another great service was in progress and a large crowd had gathered in this church building which is 28' X 64". These people can really sing and praise the Lord in worship. I asked Udjualuk to preach so the three of us shared a sermonette each with the people. Our last service ended about 9:00 and some many people thanked us for coming to Cape Dorset and invited us back as soon as possible.

May 28th. - 6:45 AM. There is broken cloud cover and the wind was quite strong. I took time to prepare breakfast. Jay and Wilf came over for breakfast and then we got a taxi for the airport. At 9:20 we were in the plane warming up the engines to take off for Frobisher Bay. At 11:20 we passed over the beam at Frobisher Bay, so we dropped down through the clouds, icing up as we descended. Five miles out, we were 3700' and did a right angle turn, but couldn't see anything. We lowered our wheels and out 12 miles we descended to 2000', going back at five miles at 800' feet we could see ground once in a while. At 11:35 we saw the runway and landed.

The weather cleared somewhat about 4:05 and we were back in the plane warming up the engines prior for take-off to Wakeham Bay (Kangiqsujuaq) in northern Quebec. We had a good chance to witness to a number of people in the airport terminal. At 5:00 we crossed the north shore of Hudson Strait and at 5:35 I could see the airstrip.

The schools are now closed for the summer holidays because they opened very early last fall. Most of the people have gone out camping so we didn't have a service tonight. Weather permitting, we plan on flying south early in the morning.

May 29th. - At 4:30 AM it was time to rise and shine and by 6:20 AM we were warming up the engines for take off to Fort Chimo. At 7:15 our instruments indicated we were passing over Payne Bay. Jay had the controls for take off, climbed up through to the top and I've been flying at 9000' since. It was eighteen degrees below zero and our heater worked good, thank the Lord. At 7:50 AM, Jay took over as we were twenty five miles from Fort Chimo and descending through heavy overcast which caused the plane to ice up badly. We landed safely and by 8:10 we were at the gas pump waiting for the gas man. There were between 400 and 500 caribou that we could see as we waited. At 8:40 AM we were ready for take-off to L.G.2. We arrived at L.G.2. at 1:05 PM nearly frozen, the heater did not work all the way and we were terribly cold even with our heavy winter parkas on. It was twenty two degrees below zero at 9000'. Hopefully our next landing will be Kitchener. At 3:35 we were 8000', just fifty two miles north of Val Dor, Quebec and our heater worked very well. At 5:45 PM we were descending to land at Kitchener airport. Thank God for a safe flight, over 1500 miles today and thank God for many souls saved during this trip, in answer to your prayers.

Chapter 12

Go Ye

Mark 16:15 "And he said unto them, Go ye into all the world and preach the gospel to every creature"

August 1st., 1990. - It was eleven degrees Celsius and time to arise and begin our trip to China. My friend Dave Kinsley arrived yesterday from Grand Rapids, Michigan to go with me. By 8:55 AM we were on the plane at the Toronto airport taxiing out to take-off. There were ten in our group with another who would join us in Hong Kong. At 9:55 we landed at Chicago O'Hare airport, 8:55 AM local time. At 11 AM Toronto time, we boarded another DC 10 plane for Seattle. We landed there at 3:55 Toronto time which was 12:55 Seattle time. We were told to hurry over to board a 747 for our 14 hour flight over the Pacific to Hong Kong. At 10 PM Toronto time we were half way across the Pacific which meant we had passed the date line, so it was Thursday, 10:00 AM. We were scheduled to land in Hong Kong at 5:30 PM local time. Rev. Ward Trotter, Pastor of the church in Apsley, Ontario, and I were seated together on all these flights and the others were scattered around. I witnessed to a few people and gave them my scripture calendars.

At 5:25 PM Hong Kong time, which is 5:25 AM in Toronto, we were descending to land. The pilot reported the temperature at twenty nine degrees Celsius. We cleared customs by 7:35 PM and four of us were in the first taxi to take us to our hotel. There we met with our representatives regarding our first trip into China and by 10:15 PM we were ready for bed.

August 3rd. - Friday at 6:30 AM it was time to get up. A thunder storm had raged for the past four hours. We had another meeting at 9:30 AM and then some of the group went shopping. At twelve noon we had a hamburger at MacDonalds. There was another meeting at 6:30 PM advising us what to take into China.

August 4th. - At 6:30 AM it was time to get moving. By 9:50 AM we were in the Hong Kong airport with all our luggage. My extra suitcase was so heavy we had to pay 620 Hong Kong dollars which is about $53.00 U.S. extra. At 10:15 we boarded the Dragon Air plane which would fly us to Beijing, the capital of China which has approximately twelve million people. At 11:20 AM I had a good time of sharing with a twenty year old university student from Italy. We landed at Beijing at 2:00 PM and were in our hotel by 3:30. There we shared with some tourists from Atlanta, Georgia.

August 5th. - Sunday, 6:00 AM. I had a good talk with two Chinese university students. I was told that many thousands were massacred in the large square a year ago last June and that more than 1100 students have been arrested, taken away in trucks and not seen again. In our hotel all rooms were bugged, cameras both inside and outside clearly visible. Our prayer is, "God save China." On the way from the airport yesterday, those in one of the taxis saw police holding young people down on the ground and handcuffing them.

At 9:05 AM I was sitting in one of the churches allowed by the government. I understand that Billy Graham preached here some time ago. A lady led the singing before the main service started. At 9:15 AM a Chinese pastor came to greet us and shake hands. At 9:30 the service started with the church and the overflow rooms packed full. "Sweet Hour of Prayer" was sung and then "Holy Holy, Holy." One of the pastors read Romans 12:1-7 and at 9:42 we all stood to sing "What a Friend we have in Jesus." A young lady took video pictures of all of us visitors. Then it was prayer time followed by the singing of "The Stranger of Galilee." Everything was in Chinese and at 10:10 another pastor preached fervently. He finished at 10:45 and the service was dismissed at 11 AM. In the evening we had a tour of the city seeing thousands of people walking all over and thousands riding on bicycles.

August 6th. - By 9 AM we were on a bus travelling to the "Great Wall of China." At 10:00 we were in a great long line of vehicles to get gasoline. We arrived at the Great Wall at 12:20 PM. I understand it is about 4000 miles long, 30 feet high and 21 feet wide at the top. Hundreds of tourists walk along the wall which I understand was completed in 221 BC. It is one of the architectural wonders of the world.

August 7th. - Beijing, China. I got up at 6.00 AM, had breakfast and at 8:05 was waiting for our bus. We were told that two Chinese Christians had been arrested - perhaps hundreds more. By 10:55 our guide had taken us to "The Temple of Heaven." Built in 1420, it is constructed with the number 9, which we are told is China's perfect number. There are 9 steps up, then a 9 square level with another 9 steps up and so on. We arrive at Tianamen Square at 1:40 PM, where the great massacre took place and the army tank damage is still visible.

August 8th. - Packed at 7:45 AM. We then toured the Emperors summer palace where he lived from May to October. It was built in 1750 AD. At 5:50 PM I visited the Canadian Embassy and the Finnish Embassy. When we visited friends in 1986, we met many of my wife's relatives, including one who now works in the Finnish Embassy here in Beijing. She has two Chinese men working in the Finnish Embassy and I had a good time sharing with them. One requested a Bible in Chinese. My Finnish friend drove me to our hotel in her Mercedes Benz and she took one of my Bibles in Chinese back with her. At 6:00 PM I was waiting for three taxis to take us to the train station.

August 9th. - 8:15 AM and we were on the train to Shanghai. It was packed full. Our group had two compartments with three bunks on each side. We slept very little. Passed rice fields with persons riding water buffalo and mud huts with thatched roofs. At 4:15 PM we arrived at Shanghai station and at 6:00 we were in the Shanghai Hotel. I understand this is the largest city in China.

August 10th. - Got up at 6:50 AM and had a good time of Bible reading, prayer and meditation. Last night I had a good opportunity to witness to a Chinese university student who speaks good English. At 5 PM we visited a fine elderly Chinese Christian couple. Before the great culture war they had a beautiful big home with a large garden but it was all confiscated. They were given a very small room in a tenement building on the third floor, using the corridor as their kitchen. They lived here since 1949. I was told there were many thousands of Christians here in Shanghai, but all 'underground'. Met other English speaking Chinese and we gave them New Testaments.

August 11th. - Had breakfast at 6:00 AM and at 8:20 was in a van driving north. We passed hundreds of people widening the highway with picks, shovels, wheel barrows and even baskets to carry the earth away. Then we drove beside a canal which is 4200 km. long It was dug out by hand about 1000 years ago. Millions of workers took ten years to build it. At 10:00 we were in the world famous silk factory where buyers come from all over the world to buy silk here. At 11:00 we visited an oriental rug factory where many girls and young men are manufacturing these rugs. I understand it takes a week for two girls to make one 2 x 3 foot rug with wonderful coloured designs. Two girls are working on a special order of a rug with human figures woven in and will cost $2000.00 U.S. At 8:20 PM we cleared customs in Shanghai airport to fly on to Hong Kong. We were on a DragonAir plane by 9:20, ready for take-off and arrived at our hotel in Hong Kong at 12:35 AM.

August 12th. - Sunday: 5:15 AM. It was time to rest. At 8:15 AM we were on a 737 DragonAir plane flying back to China with another big load of Bibles. We descended to land at Guilin at 9:15 AM. This is the land of the finger mountains. Many high mountains, like fingers, rise from a plain. At 12 noon at our air conditioned hotel it was 34 degrees Celsius. By 8:35 PM I had been able to witness to quite a few Chinese and also tourists from Canada, Italy and Australia and had given out many of my scripture calendars.

August 13th. 6:50 AM All the hotel rooms were bugged and searched. One of our group, a lady, did not go out for supper last night and was in her room when a young man walked in, was surprised and backed out. We were watched constantly. At 9:40 AM we boarded a bus with many other people on our way to a boat trip. There were many tourist boats on the Lijeang River at 11:00 AM, probably 35 or 40. We cruised down river past many little villages on both sides. I understand people have lived in these villages for thousands of years using the river for transportation. It was about a 50 mile trip.

We had a good Chinese dinner, much better than the meal on the boat which was snails and all kinds of Chinese dishes but I wasn't hungry. Arrived back in our hotel room about 8:20 PM.It was a nice trip as the river wound between many of the high finger mountains that were approximately 500 feet high. I have a good chance to witness to many.

August 14th. 7:00 AM, I had a good time of prayer and Bible reading. At 2:00 PM we took a tour inside a hollow mountain. This huge cave was over 700 feet long with hanging stalactites and stalagmites created by liquid drops. Contacts were made for our Bibles. At 10:20 PM we were on a DragonAir plane flying back to Hong Kong and we were back in our hotel at 1:30 AM.

August 15th. - 6:30 AM and it was another beautiful day "which the Lord hath made - we will rejoice and be glad in it." At 9:35 AM eleven of us were returning to China with another load of Bibles, this time by train. At 4:50 PM at customs four had made it through but seven of us were detained and our Bibles confiscated. We were told that it is illegal to take Bibles to China. I tried to reason with the officer, but in vain. We were back in our hotel in Hong Kong at 11:00 PM.

August 16th. - Time for breakfast. We had to pay for the extras - soft drinks, etc. and have 100 Hong Kong Dollars left for departure tax. By 12:20 PM we had been at the airport for over one hour trying to get through customs. Finally at 12:55 PM we boarded our 747 jet. Someone else had my seat so the stewardess took me upstairs to first class, near the crews cabin. I met the captain and after chatting with him I began to witness about Jesus. He said, "two of my crew have been working on me already." The co-pilot and the engineer were both Christians. At 2:25 PM we had been flying for one hour and were over Taiwan. I could see the mountains, cities and towns between the clouds. At 4:40 PM I saw the huge mountain in Japan on our left as it rose above the clouds. Had another good opportunity to witness to a business man sitting beside me who asked many questions regarding spiritual things. At 12:30 AM Hong Kong time, we were descending to land at Seattle. One hour later, we are sitting on a D.C. 10 plane, next to a young man enroute to join the U.S. army. I had a good talk with him and the lady on my left who seemed to be interested in spiritual things. At 8:25 AM, we were in Chicago on another D.C. 10 plane and at 11:05 PM Thursday, we landed in Toronto. It was a very rewarding trip and worth every dollar of it.

August 17th. - 2:25 AM I arrived home in Kitchener, mission accomplished.

September 29th. 1990 - After an exciting summer of meetings in churches of several denominations, where we saw many people come forward to repent of their sins and receive Jesus as Saviour, we rented our condo to a young married Chinese couple. Both have their PHD's and have just arrived in Kitchener. I told them about us taking Bibles to the Christians in China. This lady's mother is a Christian in China. I asked: "What about your father?"

"No," she said, "He is not a Christian."

I asked, "What about you two, are you Christian?"

"No," they said, "but we've been thinking about it."

So that opened the way for me to explain salvation to them and they both received Jesus as Saviour. I went out and bought them a Chinese Bible. Also, we found a good Alliance Church which had services in Chinese. Both of these young people attended this church all winter and read their Chinese Bible faithfully. They wrote us letters to Florida with all the news. After we rented our condo to the Chinese couple, we lived in our motorhome. Before we left Kitchener, the parents of the Chinese lady, flew over from China to visit them. We were invited over for a visit and the young couple interpreted for us. We had a good visit talking about the goodness of the Lord. As we were leaving, I turned to the father and asked, "Would you like to be a Christian too?"

He said "Yes." So, it was a simple matter to explain the way of salvation, and he too accepted Jesus. We left Kitchener to visit my sisters and brothers before we drove south to Florida.

October 20th. - We crossed the U.S. border at Sarnia and drove to Troy, Michigan where I preached in a very good church in both Sunday services. Many responded to the altar call, some for salvation, others to rededicate their lives to Jesus.

October 31st. - Arrived in Cape Coral, Florida after a very

good service in Lima, Ohio, Mansfield, Ohio and a few other places.

St. John 4:35-35 "Jesus saith unto them, My meat is to DO the will of Him that sent me, and to finish His work. Say not ye, There are yet four months, and then cometh harvest? Behold, I say unto you, Lift up your eyes, and look over the fields; for they are already white to harvest."

1991 Missionary trip to the Arctic

February 15th., 1991. The temperature was 66 degrees F. at 5:15 AM. As I packed the last few items, Tyyne prepared breakfast. By 8:00 I had checked through and was ready to board at the Jetport in Fort Myers. Tyyne and Daniel came with me to the airport. We were flying at 39,000 feet over Tampa in the 757 jet by 9:05 and an hour later I could see the first snow just north of Atlanta, Georgia. At 11 AM we descended to land at Detroit. Visibility was one mile in snow and we were safely on the runway at 11:30. I boarded a DC 9 for Montreal at 1:15 PM and about an hour later at 31,000', the Captain gave the weather report: temperature at Montreal was minus nineteen degrees C. We arrived there at 3:00 PM.

February 16th. - In Montreal, I got up at 5:15 AM. Yesterday I had a good chance to talk at a lady on the flight to Detroit, she was from Sarnia, Ontario. Then enroute to Montreal, I witnessed to a man from Korea. Both accepted my scripture calendar. By 8:15 AM I was on board a 737 jet plane, the temperature standing at minus 21 degrees C. I really appreciated my warm heavy underwear, my fur hat, gloves, heavy Arctic parka and flight boots. By 9:30 AM we were at 31,000' flying north. We had a hot breakfast of ham and eggs, orange juice and coffee. We landed at Fort Chimo at 11:15 AM. The Eskimo name for this place is Kuujjuaq.

February 17th. - Sunday. Yesterday I was invited to stay at a home here in Kuujjuaq, which I accepted. I'd never stayed in this home before. At 7:30 this morning I phoned home to Cape Coral, Florida and all was well there. I could see a real blizzard blowing outside and it looked very cold. Attended a local church service this morning and at 12:35 PM I enjoyed a bowl of soup. Later I went to the hospital to visit an Inuit patient on request. It remained cold with a strong wind, making the chill factor, I presume somewhere between 60 and 70 below zero. I had a precious time of prayer in the hospital, believing God to raise up this Inuit man who was dying because of a contaminated blood transfusion. It was back to the home

I was staying in about 5:30 PM and then a number of believers came in for a profitable time of Bible Study and prayer.

February 18th. - I woke up very early and had a good time of intercessory prayer. Then I had to pack my things as I wanted to make a few phone calls before plane time. Outdoors a terrific blizzard was raging, so I presumed the schools would be closed and no planes flying unless the weather changed. The 8:00 AM radio news stated that everything was closed: schools and offices. The winds were up to 40 M.P.H. and blowing snow.

February 19th, 6:30 AM. The blizzard raged all yesterday and into the night, but then it cleared and was very cold. At 11:40 AM I had a business call at one of the Quebec government offices and then I called a taxi. He got stuck in the snow, but I managed to get to the airport for my flight to Wakeham Bay. Had a good flight from Fort Chimo and at 6:20 PM I left for church for a service and I also had to perform a wedding. At 9:45 PM the church was packed full of people, many because of the wedding. The Spirit of God was present as we uplifted Jesus. I think there were nine who came forward for prayer. I then returned to the home where I was staying. As the people had to be away, I was here alone. Udjualuk left after telling me the sad story of three women who perished in the blizzard which raged through the whole north. They froze to death, but one eleven year old boy who was with them was still alive. The bodies were found today.

February 20th. - By 7:45 AM I had time to have a good hot bath and make my breakfast before anyone came to visit. It was a good day and I was able to witness and pray with some folk. By 4:30 PM, I had to get ready to go to the airport to fly to Quartaq. At 8:20 PM I was in the lovely church at Quartaq. We had landed twenty minutes ago and were ready for service. At 11:25 PM the service was over and I thank God for another good one. Many came forward for prayer.

In 1979 we built the church at Wakeham Bay and in 1980 we built here at Quartaq. The people asked me if it was possible to have a church building, just a small one about 12 X 16 would be big enough, they said. But I told them the smallest we built was 24 X 36 but they said it was too big.I sent the material up and they built the church 24 X 36. Within two years it was too small and they asked for more material to build onto the present building: 36 X 40 - so that's what we have here. God is blessing and precious souls are being saved.

February 21st. - At Quartaq at 7:30 AM Air Inuit told us their plane was full, so Udjualuk and I were on stand by. I prayed that God would help us to get to Fort Chimo. We were at the airport by 9:05 and Air Inuit promised to try and get both of us on the plane if possible, it was minus 32 degrees. We managed to get on the Twin Otter plane which was packed full of people, but it was cold even with our parkas on. We were halfway to Fort Chimo at 11:25 and 12:35 PM, I could see a few little trees as we flew south to Fort Chimo. We landed safely and I was in a home there by 1:20 PM.

February 22nd. - At 6:00 AM the temperature was 25 below zero F. which was not too bad. By 9:30 AM we were at the airport in Fort Chimo waiting for the Canadian to fly to Frobisher Bay and at 11:25 we were enroute in a 737 jet. We began our descent at 12:10 and the Captain announced it was minus 33 degrees C. We were delayed at the airport terminal getting our reservations for settlements northwest of here, north of the Arctic Circle but finally got that settled and we arrived at the parsonage which adjoins the church around 3 PM.

The presence of the Lord was great in the service as we sang His praises, and by 8:45 PM, several had given their testimonies of victory in Jesus.It concluded about 10:15 PM and was a great service with seven coming forward for prayer. God met us in a wonderful way.

February 23rd. - At 6:10 AM it was minus 33 C. Had a good time interceding for souls. Was in the airport terminal at Frobisher Bay by 7:45 AM and a little over an hour later we were on our way to Gjoa Haven. Although it was a beautiful day when we left Frobisher Bay, the weather was not so good north of the Arctic Circle. By 11:10, we were descending to land at Igloolik. Inside the airport terminal at 11:50 we could see that visibility outside was almost zero zero with a strong wind and the chill factor must have been 60 or 65 below zero, and it was freezing inside. We were still grounded in Igloolik at 2:10 PM. as blizzard conditions prevailed further north. At this point, we were more than 200 miles north of the Arctic Circle. We were finally able to get airborne and arrived at Gjoa Haven, N.W.T. at 5:25 PM, which was 3:25 PM local time as there is a two hour time difference. I stayed at the home of Matthew who was delivered from demon possession when we were here two years ago and he is praising God for His goodness. He made arrangements for a service tonight in the community hall. Many Inuits came and at 7:10 PM, just after the service began, Udjualuk led the song service and played his accordion. By 9:15 PM local time, we had enjoyed another good service and when I gave the altar call for those who wanted to give their hearts to Jesus, 15 adults came forward. I asked Udjualuk to lead them all in the sinner's prayer. Then, after the service was finished two more Inuits came to me wanting to be saved and both of them accepted Jesus. One man came on his skidoo to where I was staying and it was so very cold, with a blizzard still blowing hard and the wind chill factor about 70 below zero.

February 24th. - Sunday and I was up at 5 AM and phoned home to Florida where it was 7:00 AM. I then had a good hot bath and about 8 AM prepared some breakfast. I attended the morning worship service in the Anglican Church. At 2:10 PM we were in the community center for another great service. Two Inuits were here with video cameras to take pictures and people were gathering in. The Anglican service dismissed at 12:45 and we then got a bite to eat - caribou and rushed over. The service started at 2:15 PM and Udjualuk played his accordion and led in the singing. The mayor of Gjoa Haven played a guitar. I shared a few words of encouragement, that Jesus said, "*I will build My church, and the gates of hell shall not prevail against it.*" Udjualuk preached a powerful message and 12 responded to the altar call. The service ended about 3:55 and twenty minutes later on the way to the home where I was staying, the wind was biting cold, penetrating everything as we walked. At 8:30 PM, I had a good time of Bible Study with the man of this house and then they went on to another house for a couple of hours of singing, but I went to bed.

February 25th. - By 6:20 AM I'd had a wonderful time of intercessory prayer for the past few hours. God does hear and answer prayer. It looked very cold outside and I was very glad I didn't have to live in an igloo. At 7:00 AM in the semi-darkness I could see the neighbour loading his sled with his gun as he was going hunting. A few minutes later he started his skidoo. (I don't know how they ever start in this kind of cold weather.) He then hooked onto the long rope attached to his sled and departed. I noticed he was wearing caribou parka and pants. We came back from the Hudson Bay store at 10:15 with a few groceries which I thought would cost $25.00 to $30.00 but it was $61.89 as everything is so high priced. It was so cold out as there is a blizzard blowing with winds of 30 to 40 MPH. The wind chill factor must have been about 70 degrees below zero. At 2:10 PM an Eskimo lady came and brought a present for me to take home. It was a caribou shoulder blade which is used to stir a pot of stew or whatever. I asked her if she was a born again Christian and she told me she was one of the people saved in my meetings here two years ago, so we thank the Lord for lasting results. We had a nice time of prayer together. At 3:00 PM we had a good Bible Study on the coming of the Lord and also on the power He gives every believer to heal the sick in Jesus' Name.

At 8:15 PM I understood that our plane was delayed and we would not arrive at Spence Bay until after midnight. We were underway at 11:10 and it was a bitterly cold night with a very strong wind. At 1:10 AM we arrived at Spence Bay airport and the terminal was full of people. One lady came to me and said: "You will be staying in the same house you were in two years ago." So a man brought me there with his skidoo which was a very cold ride. Inside however, it was nice and warm and I wasn't long getting to bed.

February 26th. - 7:55 AM. Praise the Lord for another day - to do the will of God. *"Lord open my ears to listen to what the Holy Spirit is saying, open my eyes to see the fields, white unto harvest. That I will be sensitive to know and do your will."* At 2:25 PM I had been out to see about renting the community hall for a meeting tonight, but the person in charge could not be found, so I returned to the home where I was staying. A fierce blizzard was blowing with strong winds, drifting snow and cold temperatures. Things worked out however and at 6:45 PM I was in a brand new recreation complex which had an indoor skating rink and the community center. The mile and a half ride on skidoo was cold and we looked to the Lord for a good meeting. By 7:20 PM, quite a crowd had gathered in and I asked the Anglican minister, Rev. Fred Birmingham, to open the service with a few words of welcome and prayer. The gospel was then preached and nine came forward for prayer. We thank the Lord for the working of the Holy Spirit in these hearts.

February 27th. - 7:30 AM. Another day to seek the lost. I've been interceding for the people here at Spence Bay, that God will pour out His Holy Spirit upon them and that many will turn to Jesus and be saved. Had a good time of Bible reading and prayer in the home where I was staying and then about 9:30 AM, I visited another home. The people were hungry for God. One lady had headaches for a very long time. Jesus touched her in answer to prayer and now she said her headaches were all gone. Praise the Lord!. By 2:20 PM we had visited many homes, prayed for bed-ridden people and other sicknesses. Many expressed their appreciation that we took time to visit and pray for them. I had already shared the Word of the Gospel and Udjualuk was preaching in our service in the Anglican Church at 9:20 PM and a good crowd came. It ended about 10:45 PM and I believe 24 came forward for prayer at the altar call. I froze my nose walking back to the house.

February 28th. - We are to leave for Pelly Bay this morning and I finished breakfast of coffee and bannock at 8:30 AM. The folk here told me they came home at 2:30 this morning. They had Udjualuk hold another service in a home. Thank God for these Eskimos with a strong desire to serve the Lord. They have asked for a Full Gospel Church here.

Arrived at the airport at 9:50 PM and the weatherman said it was 42 degrees below. Was on the 748 plane to Pelly Bay at 11:20 and arrived at 1:40 PM. I spoke to two white men who are working here about the gospel story. No response visibly, but the seed has been sown. Udjualuk visited an Eskimo family while I tried to get the community hall for a meeting tonight and at 4:35 PM I checked into the "only" hotel in town - $110. per night. I had a bowl of soup, a sandwich and coffee - $15. Met a few folk down "town" and was able to witness for Jesus. 7:40 PM I finished preaching the gospel in the only church in Pelly Bay, the Catholic Church. Udjualuk and I went out visiting until 10:15 PM and had a wonderful opportunity to witness to one of the white schoolteachers and his wife. I explained the born again experience and I am sure the Holy Spirit is working in their hearts.

March 1st., 1990 - I find that intercessory prayer accomplishes great changes. Shut doors have been opened, hard hearts softened; indifference turned to hunger for spiritual things and a greater desire for the Word of God and prayer. I completed a $10. breakfast at 8:30 AM as the cook was late coming in. It was 46 degrees below, plus the wind chill factor. We visited quite a few people by 8:15 PM but it seems the devil has most of these people in bondage and fear. Made a little headway with the Inuit and had a nice visit with a Christian nurse and another visit and supper with a young couple, he teaches here; they are from Newfoundland.

March 2nd. - Up at 6:10 AM and we plan to fly to Igloolik this morning. At 6:40 AM I watched 13 caribou from the hotel window as they pawed the snow off the ground and ate the moss and grass. We were in the airport terminal at 10:45 AM and the airplane was late, expected at 11:15. Temperature was 48 degrees below zero but there was very little wind. We boarded the 748 turbo plane to Igloolik and arrived there at 12:55 PM. Peter, the pastor and his wife met us at the airport. At this point we changed our watch two hours ahead to 2:55 PM. At 6:50 PM we were in our church, praying and interceding for the meeting. We had a great service which ended about 9:15 with many around the altar seeking God. God is so good. Quite a few Christians gathered here in the pastor's home where they enjoyed eating raw frozen Arctic Char fish. I said "Good night" and went to bed.

March 3rd. - Sunday, 11 AM the morning worship service began and many people gathered in spite of the 40 degrees below zero temperature. We sang a number of choruses including "Hallelujah" and "Oh Happy day when Jesus washed my sins away" in the Eskimo language. One of the new converts gave her testimony in the wonderful service which lasted until

12:50 PM. The people here were not afraid to praise the Lord with a loud voice, hands raised to heaven, and some with tears of joy on their faces. Udjualuk preached a great message in line with what I preached last night. At 2 PM he was on the local radio station preaching the gospel. Prepared to go to church about 6:10 PM and it was 42 degrees below zero. This is the church that Sanford Trotter of Apsley provided much of the material. Different ones gave their testimony including the pastor's wife and the church was pretty well filled. You should have heard them singing the praise of God. Praise the Lord for His many blessings. As I gave the altar call, many came up for prayer, several with tears flowing down their faces, crying to the Lord. There must have been at least 30 at the altar.

March 4th. - 6:55 AM I was packing and getting ready to go as some said the plane gets in early today. On the turbo jet to Frobisher Bay and hopefully to Cape Dorset at 10:30 AM. Met a Christian nurse who worked at the Radar base and had a good time sharing the good things of God. At 12:55 PM they served a good hot meal and I was able to witness to a Catholic employee of First Air. He was very interested in spiritual things and I also had a time of sharing the good news with an Anglican Inuit. I believe the seed sown fell on good ground. Once in a while I could see the ground or frozen water as we were flying at 31,000 feet. We touched down at Frobisher Bay at 1:25 PM and had to taxi to the terminal. At 5:10 PM I boarded the plane for Cape Dorset but the plane was so full that Udjualuk couldn't get a seat and had to wait for the Wednesday flight.

By 7 PM I was in Cape Dorset thawing out from the skidoo ride from the airport up and down sharp hills and around curves with the wind blowing and snow coming down. The heat in this warm house was welcome. Was in the church by 7:15 PM as the people had announced a service for tonight. This is the church we built in 1978 and is so beautiful, nice and clean. I didn't even have time to change my clothes and the service was underway with two men playing guitars, one on drums and a sister leading in the singing. It was a great service and the presence of the Lord was so real. We had a great time of prayer and many came forward for a touch from the Lord. They are so happy that they can have a service every night.

March 5th. - Spent early morning studying and praying for tonight's service. At 10.00 AM I went to the Hudson Bay store to buy a few groceries. Canned milk $1.09, loaf of bread $3.73, 2 kg. sugar $4.42, 1 doz. eggs $4.07, 1 lb. margarine $2.54, very small jar of coffee $2.97, macaroni and cheese $1.46, 1/2 lb. sausage $4.26, 1 lb. bacon $6.23, etc. etc. Things are much more expensive in the Co-Op store. The temperature was around 40 to 42 degrees below and after visiting a few homes, I decided about 1:20 PM to prepare for tonight's meeting. At 6:00 PM I went to the church to intercede for souls to be saved. God gave us another good meeting which ended about 9:45 PM and the Holy Spirit worked in many hearts, to come forward for prayer. A number were there who had not attended for a long time and God moved by His Holy Spirit as we interceded for the Cape Dorset population.

March 6th. The weather at 7:20 AM was very windy and blowing snow, a real blizzard and I thought there would be no plane today. I made and finished breakfast by 8:30 AM and the blizzard seemed twice as bad as before. The bulldozers worked to open roads for the school busses and the blizzard raged on. I never thought a plane would land here in this weather, but at 11:05 AM one did and Udjualuk was on it. One of the Inuit Christians has a truck and he brought us to the village. I stopped at the store and he brought Udjualuk to where he was staying. I bought a few more groceries for Udjualuk and then walked back. By 1.10 PM it was a complete blizzard. We couldn't even see across the road. It was a good thing the plane came this morning. Spent time praying and interceding for souls and then returned to the church at 6:15 PM to pray and intercede more. The blizzard continued raging in all its fury and the Anglican church announced on the local radio station that there wouldn't be a service in their church tonight because of the storm. Because of the blizzard, we had only about half a crowd but thank God for those brave people who weathered the storm to come and worship. Udjualuk preached and at 8:45 PM eight came forward to be filled with the Holy Spirit. I don't think I've ever seen such a blizzard, the wind must have been 50 or 60 miles per hour. I thank God for those who came to hear the Word of God preached.

March 7th. - 6:55 AM and the storm was over and it was a beautiful day. The snowplow was busy opening the streets. I returned to where I was staying at 2 PM as Udjualuk and I had visited quite a few homes where we prayed for elderly and sickly people. We also went to the local radio station and preached the gospel to the whole village. In some homes we had tea and bannock and the last home we had an extra treat of pieces of caribou fat with bannock. I found out the plane schedule had been changed from Saturday to Friday, so I'll have to prepare to leave tomorrow. Was in the church for another service by 6.25 PM and we had the biggest crowd yet with the church almost filled. The Bible text was Eph. 6:10 - 18 and other scriptures. Many came forward for prayer to be better soul winners, overcomers and intercessors. God is doing a great work here in Cape Dorset and all across the Arctic.

March 8th. - By 7:35 AM I've had a precious time of prayer and intercession for the people of Cape Dorset, that God will pour out His Holy Spirit upon them, to save them and prepare them for the soon coming of Jesus Christ. Then I got up to prepare and eat breakfast and pack to fly to Frobisher Bay. It was snowing out but not bad flying weather. I returned to the village at 12:25 PM. I had prepared for the flight at 11 and rushed to the airport only to find the plane delayed till 2 PM. At 5 PM the plane still hadn't arrived but did shortly after and I was on board ready for take off at 5:25 PM. I was in the parsonage at Iqaluit (Frobisher Bay) at 7:45 PM. The Inuit pastor and his wife met me at the airport. They arrived by skidoo but I had one heavy suitcase and another heavy box, so the pastor's wife and I took a taxi, and the pastor came by skidoo almost as fast as the taxi. The parsonage is part of the church building, but no one is living here so it's quiet and nice to study and pray.

March 9th. 5:30 PM. I've had a wonderful day here - myself and the Lord - a time to intercede and pray for the services tomorrow. I also went down to the airport terminal and purchased a ticket for Udjualuk's plane trip home - nearly $700.00. Then I went to the Hudson Bay store and bought groceries to last me here till I leave at noon on Tuesday. My last two Inuit visitors just left. We had a lovely visit and a time of prayer together. More visitors came through the evening and the last four left about 9:10. We thank God for what He is doing in the hearts of the people.

March 10th. - Sunday, 7:10 AM. I've just phoned home to find out how things are and let them know I am fine here. It's quite mild weather, only minus 18 degrees instead of 40 or 50 below zero. 11:35 AM I sensed such a real presence of the Lord in the morning worship service, and at 12:45 PM we thank God for honouring His Word, as Timothy the Inuit lawyer, interpreted for me. These folk are so appreciative of good Bible teaching and many of them take down notes and scripture references. At 6:45 PM we were back in the church praying for the service. One of the Inuit brothers went out yesterday morning to hunt. He saw many caribou but only needed one, so now he brought me a good piece of caribou for tomorrow. It was a great service ending about 8:55 PM. A number of strangers attended along with the Christians. A good response as I gave the altar call - twelve came forward for prayer.

March 11th. This morning at 6:00 it was 20 degrees below zero. I cut some caribou steaks and fried them for breakfast.

Mm-mm, was that caribou steak ever delicious! If you've never had a caribou steak for breakfast, you don't know what you're missing. I phoned the weather station and was told the temperature should warm up to 16 degrees below zero, by the afternoon. By 10:45 AM I'd been downtown to get an export permit to take Arctic Char and caribou meat south. With the wind chill factor the weather office says it's more than 40 degrees below zero. I had a good opportunity to witness to the Inuit wild life officer and then the big husky white man boss came in, so I witnessed to him and found he is a Christian from Newfoundland. By 3:40 PM I'd been out visiting a few homes, after a time of prayer and intercession. It was still 20 below zero with a 30 mile per hour wind, which makes it quite cold, especially when walking and facing the wind. Frobisher Bay is a very needy place, and needs a great move of God, which I believe will take a lot of intercessory prayer and witnessing. The Christians here have asked for your prayers. At 8:30 PM I had been out visiting again. The last home was a tragedy. The husband, a white man, walked out on his wife and her two children last September and left a big mortgage on their home plus many other bills. She asked, why - why - all this had come upon her. She even felt the Lord had forsaken her. We had Bible reading and prayer and I encouraged her to trust the Lord and not give up. No wonder the Lord laid the burden of intercessory prayer upon me. Now I know the reason. God help us to be obedient to His leading.

March 12th. - At 6:30 AM it was 29 degrees below zero and a 30 mile per hour wind. The weather office said it was 55 below zero with the wind chill factor. I'd had a good time of prayer by 11:40 AM, interceding for the people of Frobisher Bay, that souls will be saved. Made myself an early lunch of caribou steak. Temperature went up to 26 below. Arrived at 1:05 to the airport terminal in Frobisher Bay. A blizzard was blowing and some flights had been cancelled.One of the Christian men from Broughton Island, who was the mayor there, came over and we had an enjoyable time of fellowship. By 1:40 PM I was on the jet for Montreal and at 7:20 PM had settled in a Motel in Montreal. I phoned our youngest son David who lives in Ottawa to meet me at the Montreal airport to pick up a good size polar bear stone carving which he ordered two years ago.. We had a nice visit together before he left for Ottawa. Was tired and planned to go to bed early. I had a good long talk with one of the stewardesses on the plane. She appeared very interested to learn of spiritual things. We must pray that the seed sown will germinate and bring forth fruit.

March 13th. 6 AM in the Montreal motel. I've finished reading the Bible through once again, so my morning reading was in Genesis 1. By 7:45 AM I'd had a good time of prayer and intercession and ready to go to the airport. Was in the airport terminal and had cleared customs by 8:35 AM and was waiting to board Northwest flight to Detroit and Fort Myers. Had a good discussion with a skier from Ottawa who was going to Colorado. He admitted he was not a born again Christian but appeared interested. It really felt good to take off my heavy long underwear, my big flight boots, fur hat and heavy parka. It made me feel so light. The temperature here was zero degrees. By 10:30 AM we were passing over the finger lakes area of New York State. I couldn't see any snow on the ground and the lakes were free of ice. The jet was a 727. By 10:40 we were flying over Lake Erie and open water. I did see some snow on the ground and an ice covered lake so it must have been higher elevation. I had a little talk with a business man two seats away and then he began typing on his computer. We landed at 11:15 in Detroit. A beautiful day, 35 F. By 11:45 I was on the plane for Fort Myers. I just had time to get off the one plane and find the gate for my next flight, and they were boarding so I got right on. We landed at Fort Myers at 3:15 PM. Had a good talk to the lawyer beside me from Chicago. He appeared interested as I shared the gospel message with him. Pray that the seed sown will germinate and grow. I thank all those who made this trip possible, by your prayers and financial support. Each of you will share in the rewards at that day when Jesus comes, which I believe is very soon. God bless you all.

April 2nd., 1991 - Started our trip north. Visited a few of our friends including Alf and Mae Huntley in Clearwater, Florida, also Vicki Lewis who was with our group to Israel. She would like to make her first trip to Canada to visit us, which eventually she did the last part of July and the first part of August, 1991.

May 18th., 1991 - We travelled north to Kirkland Lake and took part in our granddaughter's wedding, when Dawn Adams and Thomas Dekker were united in marriage. It was a beautiful wedding and many loved ones and friends attended.

Chapter 13

Redeeming the Time

Ephesians 5:15 - 17 "See then that ye walk circumspectly, not as fools, but as wise, Redeeming the time, because the days are evil. Wherefore be ye not unwise, but understanding what the will of the Lord is."

1991 Arctic Trip

June 12th., 1991 - Kitchener Ontario, 4:30 AM. Time to get up and get going. It was 17 degrees C. Arrived Toronto terminal at 7 AM and by 9:30 was enroute to Montreal. At 9:50 I was having a good talk with an oil executive business man next to me. He said he lived only for today - but I pray the seed sown will germinate and grow.

At 11:35 AM I was on board a 727 jet which flies from Montreal to Kuujjuaq, formerly known as Fort Chimo. I had a good opportunity to share the gospel with two men in the airport. Although I can't report that either accepted the Lord, I feel good that I was able to sow the good seed of God's Word. By 1:30 PM I could see snow and ice through the clouds on the ground as we flew north. At 2:50 I was in Kuujjuaq in the Co-Op Hotel. My baggage did not come and the next plane is tomorrow afternoon before my luggage can arrive. I have to make the best of the situation. There are two hotels here, the Kuujjuaq Hotel at $165.00 per night or the Co-Op Hotel at $96.60 per night. It was 3 degrees C at 9:55 PM. I bought a few things to eat at the Hudson Bay store and I noticed quarts of fresh strawberries at $5.97 compared to .99 cents in Kitchener.

June 13th. - Time to rise and shine at 6:45 and the temperature is 1 degree C. I had a good talk with a man from Montreal yesterday, who also stayed here last night. He appeared interested in what the Bible says. At 9:10 AM I went to a restaurant for coffee with the same young man I talked to yesterday. He said that the temperatures were below freezing and cold before spring's good weather arrived three days ago. Again this morning I had another good talk with him about salvation and the Christian life.

By 10:55 AM I've been over to the town hall office and had a good visit with the assistant Mayor and had prayer with him. A few years ago he accepted Jesus, but has had very little

Christian fellowship because there are no Christian meetings here. One Inuit lady is saved but not her husband. My friend had tears in his eyes as we parted. I plan to see him again before I leave. I've just received word that my luggage has been found in Montreal and hopefully will be on the flight here this afternoon. At 3 PM I found that my luggage had arrived so I can dress warm, thank the Lord. I returned from the High School graduation exercises at 6:50 PM. Eight students completed and passed 12th grade. Also a professor from a University in China came in today. I had a good long talk with him and he asked me for an English New Testament, which I gave him.

June 14th. - At 6:30 it was zero degrees and a nice sunny day. I had a good hot shower and a time of prayer, then I went out for a walk. At 8:20 AM the weather station reported a low of minus 6 degrees near midnight. I met a young man 31 years old and had a good talk with him about Jesus. He prayed the sinner's prayer asking forgiveness and invited Jesus into his heart. By 11:30 I was in the Fort Chimo airport ready to depart for George River. I was told that they are expecting me to preach in the Anglican Church at 7 PM. I was in the lovely Anglican Church by 6:55 and people were gathering in for the service which lasted until 10:00 PM. What a wonderful service. We only had one chorus and sang it twice, had prayer and then they turned it over to me. I preached on "what is the will of God for your life". When I gave the altar call, everyone came forward and knelt down to receive Jesus Christ as Saviour. I believe a very few were saved in the past, but now so many made a commitment of their lives to Jesus. They asked for another service tomorrow night.

June 15th. - 11:45 AM. I've been out all morning, exploring this lovely village and talking with the Inuits I met. Some were repairing their boats or canoes, to be ready when the ice goes out. Ice 6 and 7 feet thick fills this bay off the George River. There is much snow on the side of the mountains yet, which they say most of it will be melted by the end of July. The tide comes up river from Ungava Bay and fills this bay once every twelve hours.

I brought a big suitcase full of good clothing to give to the families and in the afternoon many women gathered to pick out the clothing they needed. At 5:45 I was in a neighbour's house where they were having a birthday party. One of the girls is 17 today and there was so much to eat - all cooked meats, goose, caribou, seal, plus potatoes, peas and carrots. Many people were here and I had a Canada goose leg, potatoes, peas and carrots. My interpreter Sophie was called to the nursing station for an emergency as a man had been brought in with severe food poisoning, so our meeting had to be cancelled as no one else could interpret.

June 16th. - Sunday. 9:50 AM and we were in the Anglican Church for the morning service. At 11:55 we praise the Lord for another opportunity to proclaim the Good News of the Gospel to a church full of people. I understand that no one from the "outside" has ever been here before to preach the gospel. So I thank God for this privilege. My interpreter said that many came to her and expressed their appreciation for this message. At 6:45 PM I was back in the church for the evening services as people gathered in while the organist played. It was another wonderful service ending at 9:15. A few more came up for prayer, some for salvation, healing and to receive the baptism of the Holy Spirit. Then it was time for the young people's service which ended about 10:55 PM. I was tired having preached three times today, but I felt very rewarded to see how the people responded.

June 17th. 5:45 AM and very foggy. I didn't expect the plane to come in this kind of weather. By 2:35 the weather cleared and we were sitting in the Twin Otter plane ready to fly to Fort Chimo. Thirty minutes later we were at about 5000 feet and all the lakes are still frozen over. I watched caribou running over the tundra. Arrived at the Co-Op Hotel in Fort Chimo at 5:05 PM. While in the George River airport terminal I had an interesting talk with a middle aged man who believed that he would be allowed into Heaven because he was good. He listened to me as I shared the Word of God and asked me many questions. It seems as if it was the first time he ever heard the way of salvation explained. He is a white man living at George River for many years. I believe he married an Inuit woman.

June 18th. Got up about 6:00 AM. The weather was overcast but flyable. I've had a good time of prayer and intercession for the last couple of hours. The taxi should soon be here to take me to the airport. I boarded the twin Otter plane and at 7:35 and we had climbed through the overcast and were on top in beautiful sunshine flying to Quaqtaq. The taxi didn't come, but another fellow had a half ton truck. He took me to the airport so I had a good talk with him and he was glad to receive a New Testament from me. Arrived in Quaqtaq at 10:30 AM. The police man met me at the airport and brought me to the pastor's home. The pastor is away at his camp and his wife is teaching at the school. I was hungry so I found some eggs, bread, butter and jam and I had a late breakfast. In these homes they expect us to make ourselves at home and eat what is available if we are hungry. 3:25 PM. Many people are out camping, some 10 miles out, 30 miles and even 60 miles. They travel with a skidoo and there is plenty of snow, even in the village. The pastor's wife is a school teacher and she finishes her duties today at 3:00 PM for the school season. One of our Christian men is the Co-Op store manager, and has been for many years. Two of our men are the village police officers. The Mayor is one of our Christian Inuit women. Others have important jobs.

The service was on by 7:05 and more people gathered in as we sang.The pastor's wife led the singing with a loud voice and the Mayor of Quaqtaq played the organ while one of the men played his guitar. It was another good service and it ended at 10:05 PM. A good crowd attended and God blessed as a number came forward for prayer. This is whale season and the hunters got two whales today. Most of the women in the village gathered in one place to eat whale meat.

June 19th.At 6:30 AM it was another beautiful sunny day. Each night it freezes, but by the afternoon the snow melts and the water runs. The 7:45 AM radio weather report said the temperatures were much above normal. Normal low would be 10 below at night and 4 or 5 above during the day, but now it goes to 10 to 12 above in the afternoon. At 9:50 AM I was in the police station where one of our men was on duty. The pastor took me to the house where they ate the raw whale meat after the service last night. It looked like blubber or fat to me. By 2:30 PM I was on a 748 turbo jet plane to Sugluk at 9000 feet flying west along the Hudson Strait. Arrived in Noah Isaac's home at 5:15 PM. We were invited to the evening service in the Anglican Church. It's been a few years since I was here last, but quite a few people came to greet and welcome me. But many of the people I knew were out camping as in other villages. God blessed in a special way in the service which ended at 10:00 PM. The Anglican minister interpreted for me. When I gave the altar call, 9 people came forward for prayer. They asked for another service tomorrow night, if I'm still here. The sun was still shining bright even after 10 o'clock.

June 20th. - Another beautiful sunny day. At 7:30 AM Noah had already gone to work on his 45 ft. Peter Head boat. The fiord here is still full of ice and the people are still using skidoos. I was out all morning, visiting and witnessing with a few families. The announcement came over the local radio at 2 PM that we would have another service in the church tonight. I returned to my room at 2:25 PM and as I prepared for tonight's service, from my window I could see 4 skidoos pulling sleds, arrive on the ice in the fiord. They were returning from fishing camp. By 4 PM the Canadian North Television officer had just completed an interview with me regarding our missionary work in the Arctic which will be shown later in the year on TV. By

10:10 PM the TV officer had televised most of the Bible Study we held in the church tonight. A few came forward for prayer after the Bible Study.

June 21st. - 7:30 AM. Another sunny day. Dogs have been howling all across the village. Some of the Inuit have returned to dog teams now instead of skidoos. I saw the tide waters were high this morning and the ice was beginning to break up along the shore. By 9:40 AM I was away down the coast of the fiord, sitting on a sled which was hooked to a skidoo. There are 20 to 30 skidoos here up on shore till next fall. Yet there are still quite a few families operating their skidoos, going out to camp, most of them will pitch a tent in a week or so. I noticed the ice turning a dark colour which indicates it is getting thin and dangerous to travel on, so I believe all skidoos will be brought in, in a few days. I saw 2 skidoos arrive about 7:30 AM but the men left them off shore while they came to get groceries and go back to camp, toward the Hudson Strait. By 12:20 I've had a wonderful morning sharing Jesus with others. One fine middle age couple prayed the sinner's prayer. Was back at the airport at 4:05 PM buying my ticket to fly to Ivujivik. At 7:15 PM we were flying at 4000' and should be landing at Ivujivik in about 15 minutes. Hudson Strait seemed to be full of ice as far as I could see.

Pastor Peter and a few of the Christians met me at the airport at 9:50 PM. He said he had booked a room for me at the hotel where I would be more quiet. He explained that this is hunting season for whales and geese and the men hunt till 1:00 and 2:00 in the morning and they didn't want me disturbed. At the hotel was a kitchen where we could cook and eat. The Co-Op store was closed when we arrived, but they opened it so that I could buy some groceries. There is much open water here and I can see hunters coming in with many Canada geese. Pastor Peter said they got two whales yesterday and hoped to get more tonight which they would divide between the whole village. This village is on the point where the Hudson Bay and Hudson Strait meet. We built a church here a few years ago.

June 22nd. Overcast and much cooler at 7:50 AM. By 9:55 AM I've had a nice walk all through the village, praying and interceding for those people for whom Jesus suffered and died. I only met one man who was working on a large soap stone carving. I believe this was the coldest day of the whole trip so far, with a strong wind blowing and at times a drizzle. I was so glad to have my heavy parka with a fur lined hood which I've been wearing each day. At 3:05 PM Peter came running into the hotel calling me: "The whales are coming, come and see the whale hunt!" Hunters were gathering with heavy rifles. I saw two whales surface, a man shot and got the two. Then two more came and they shot them. A canoe went out and towed the 12 foot whale in to shore.More whales came and they got three more. I asked Peter: "What will you do with all this meat?" He explained; "We give every family as much as they need, and we put the rest in freezers for later." Peter cut about an inch strip off two flippers and he then cut about a one inch piece for me. I ate it and swallowed it, my first taste of whale. All this was happening right behind the hotel, so I could even see from my window. Even with my parka on it was very cold, standing still. By 4:35 PM, eight whales were shot and I helped pull some up on shore. Most of the people came right down and began cutting, eating and really enjoying the feast. The sun came out and the clouds moved away and it turned into a beautiful afternoon as I returned to pray for the meetings in the church.

Because of cutting up whales, we were asked to start our meeting at 9 o'clock in our lovely Ivujivik church. By 9:05 quite a few gathered and more were coming in.It was a great service with a very good crowd and ended about 11:10 PM. Many came up for prayer and God blessed in a wonderful way.

June 23rd. - Sunday. I always phone home every Sunday morning about 7 AM. Arrived at the church at 10:30 AM to pray and intercede for souls in the 1 o'clock meeting. Had a good meeting this morning and these Inuit really worship the Lord in spirit and in truth and put their whole heart into their worship. I made reservations to fly to Povungnituk tomorrow. At 5 PM a couple came to visit me at the hotel. I visited Maggie Kristensen, police constable and her mother Peta. Arrived in church at 5:45 for the 6 o'clock meeting. At 8:10 PM I praise the Lord for all His blessings and goodness to us! Many came forward for prayer, to seek the Lord for more of His fullness during the altar call. God is raising up a pure, clean, holy army of people among the Inuit people.

June 24th. 3 PM. The truck will soon come to take me to the airport. Peter the pastor has just left to get some whale meet for me to take to Povungnituk. He told me how glad he was with the results of these meetings and the number of men and women who came up for salvation. One woman especially, never came to church, only once at the dedication service. She came last Saturday and again on Sunday and was one of the ones who came to receive Jesus, Praise the Lord!

At 6:20 PM we were still sitting in the plane on the airstrip, the fog was very bad. Finally they decided to take off and at 7:40 PM we were descending to land at Povungnituk. I wondered if the people would still want a service. It was a long time since I'd eaten but I could wait. At 9:15 I was in our church for a service and our lady pastor asked if I was too tired. I said, "No, I'm ready now. So here we are". It ended at 11:10 and not too many came out at such short notice. But God blessed in a wonderful way. Two came forward for salvation and the Christians were encouraged to see a move of God. Many were out camping as in the other villages.

June 25th. - By 3:05 PM, I'd been out visiting the homes and in the hospital where we prayed for two sick Inuit. Then I prepared for the evening service. At 6:45 I was in the church for another service which lasted till 10:30. These people really love to sing and praise the Lord. Quite a number, perhaps 15 or 16 came forward for prayer. Then we went to the home where I stay and a couple who attended the service was there. About 10:50 PM another lady came in to visit, but as I had to get up at 6 AM, I excused myself and went to bed.

June 26th. 5:55 AM brought a beautiful sunny day. By 6:40 I'd made and eaten breakfast and then phoned my friend, an Inuit who is acting Mayor of Povungnituk, to come with his 4 wheeler and took me to the airport. At 8:15 AM we were late taking off in the twin Otter but by 8:20 we were off and flying to Umiujaq. Hudson Bay was full of ice and by 8:55 we were flying over thousands of lakes. Some of them were open, others had ice. I was told they were full of Arctic Char and lake trout. We descended at 9:55 AM through heavy fog to land at Umiujaq. We'd been flying over the fog for the last 35 minutes. At last at 10:10 AM we were on the landing strip. I didn't like that fog at all!

At 1:15 PM I was in our little church where the night meeting was scheduled for 7 PM. As soon as the plane took off this morning after I arrived, the fog closed in completely, right down to the ground and remained the same all day so I thank the Lord I was able to get here.

At 2:10 PM another plane was scheduled to come in but all flights have been cancelled and the airport closed, due to the fog which is right down to the ground. At 6:05 I was in the church interceding for souls to be saved. Quite a number gathered by 7:35 for the service. The acting Mayor, who also serves as the police constable, played the guitar for music as we sang hymn after hymn worshipping the Lord. Ending at 10 PM, it was another great meeting with a fairly good crowd and sincerity in praise and worship. Nine came forward for prayer after the message. All in all, we had a precious time together for the glory of God.

June 27th. At 6:50 AM, Willie, my Inuit brother in whose home I am staying, hollered, "The world news is coming, come and see the TV." It was a cold rain all morning. I visited a few homes to encourage the Christians. At 12:25 PM I returned to

Willie's home to get lunch for myself. Willie was away. A few minutes later an Inuit woman came in with an armful of clothes to wash in Willie's washer. She told me she was in our Full Gospel Church for the first time last night. She did not go forward to receive Jesus, but wanted to be born again and ready for Jesus' coming. She then accepted Jesus and was born into the family of God. Praise the Lord! By 4:05 I returned to Willie's house from visiting. The fog was so heavy, visibility was down to 200 yards. Went to the church at 6:00 PM to intercede for souls. 7:05 PM another wonderful service was underway. After praise and worship, different ones gave their testimony, while the acting Mayor interpreted for me. It ended at 10:50 and God blessed in the service. Many came up for prayer and some new people attended. After I returned to Willie's house, 2 Inuit women, both of them backsliders, who had not attended the service, requested prayer to be restored to the Lord.

June 28th. - At 7:05 AM Willie had the World News on again. It was quite foggy outside and the temperature was 4 degrees C. By noon I'd been out visiting homes, praying for the sick and encouraging the people. Then I got lunch and prepared for the plane at 1:00 o'clock. We were on the plane and on our way at 2:15 PM.

We landed at Akulivik and took off again at 5:40 PM. I could see 9 caribou feeding beside the runway. I suppose they are used to planes landing and taking off. I met an Inuit friend whom I hadn't seen for at least 10 years. He lives here and asked that I come and hold services as soon as possible. But my schedule didn't permit me to stop on this trip. At 8:40 we were still flying, but near my destination, Kangirsuk on Payne Bay and by 9:25 PM I was in pastor Peter Airo's home.

June 29th. - 7:50 AM. I got up and found enough food for breakfast. Then Peter got up and made his own breakfast. He lives alone and is middle age and a good pastor. Last night I had visitors until midnight. They could speak English, but Peter does not. So Peter and I are batching together and get along fine, even though he speaks very limited English. I returned from visiting all morning at 12:15 PM. I met some very nice Inuit people. Peter worked on his big boat, a 36' long Peter Head. Went to our lovely church about 6:45 PM. People were gathering in. We built here in 1982. There was quite a good turnout tonight in spite of so many out camping, fishing and hunting. A few came up for prayer and two young men around 20 years old prayed the sinners prayer. Both of them and Vicky, my interpreter came over to Peter's house to discuss more of the Bible.

June 30th. - Sunday. Peter left at 6:30 AM to put the oil

stove on in the church. We had to have it on for the service last evening too. There is still a lot of snow drifts on the ground and much floating ice in the bay. I arrived at the church at 9:15 AM. It was nice and warm, but I wore my heavy parka as I do every day.. I asked Pastor Peter when and where he had accepted Jesus as Saviour. Before we built the church here in Payne Bay in 1982, we had already built a church in Wakeham Bay in 1979. He travelled to Wakeham Bay, attended our church services and accepted Jesus. Praise the Lord! The service started at 10:00 AM and they sang a few choruses and turned the service to me to preach. Then the Pastor spoke. We could sense the presence of God in this place as He spoke to us through His Word.

7:00 PM. The evening service has started and the people were gathering in. Some of us came in at 6:00 to pray and intercede for souls. There was a much bigger crowd tonight and God touched many souls. The service ended at 9:55 and we thank the Lord for the moving of the Holy Spirit.

July 1st., 1991 - 6:50 AM. Another beautiful sunny day, but the north wind is very cold. Peter went to work on his boat early and I did some visiting and witnessing for Jesus by 10:15 AM. What a joy to lead a soul to Jesus. 2:15 PM. I've just returned from the Canada Day celebration on the next hill west of town: races, javelin throwing, tea making and a raw seal party - (I'm glad I had my dinner at 11:30 AM). But I've had many good opportunities to witness for Jesus. Some said they accepted Jesus a few years ago, but are now walking afar off. I encouraged them to draw closer to the Lord. Peter brought home two fresh Arctic Char from the waters of Payne Bay and we finished a big meal of Arctic Char. Then I went to the airport to fly to Fort Chimo. By 9:20 we were descending to land at Fort Chimo and at 10:55 PM I was in a nice Inuit home with a lovely couple.

July 2nd. 7;15 AM. Praise the Lord for another sunny day. At 10:30 AM I was back to the airport at Fort Chimo waiting to fly to Frobisher Bay -Iqaluit. At 11:30 PM we were taxiing out for take off on the 747 Jet. An Inuit lady called, "Hello John." They are a couple that I had performed a wedding for a few years ago in Frobisher Bay. Looking out of the plane at 11:40, I can see that Ungava Bay is full of ice. I understand it will not be open till late August for ships to bring in supplies. The Captain reported at 12:10 PM that we are flying at 33,000' and the temperature at Frobisher Bay is a nice warm 14 degrees C.

By 1:30 PM I arrived in our little church "Faith Alive". Then I went to the store to get a few things as I plan on being here until Thursday. In the evening, the Inuit pastor came over and we had a nice visit and a time of prayer. Then, about 8:25 PM I visited a family.

July 3rd. - At 6:50 AM I discovered it's cold. The furnace quit working some time during the night. I got up, make breakfast and a cup of hot coffee. The temperature really was not so cold - 8 degrees C.

8:10 AM. It's about 58 years ago that God called me to "go north and preach the gospel", but where? The north is so large. At first I thought it may be Greenland. So I wrote a letter to the government of Greenland, stating my intentions of doing missionary work in that land. I waited many weeks for an answer. The government of Greenland sent my letter to the King of Denmark. At long last, the letter arrived from the king's secretary, in which he stated his appreciation of my concern and interest for the people of Greenland. The letter stated that their state church (Lutheran) was well able to look after the spiritual needs of the people of Greenland, and that the country was closed to outside missionaries. So that door was closed. But God led me to northern Canada - as far north as the last Inuit settlement nearest the North Pole in the Canadian Arctic.

As most of the Inuit people here in Frobisher Bay are away hunting, fishing and camping, there will be no services here so I decided to make reservations to fly to Greenland, as it is not far east of Baffin Island where I am now. By 12:30 PM I've been out visiting and met some wonderful people; had prayer and encouraged them in the Lord. By 12:50 PM I'd finished a little lunch. I noticed the price on a few groceries I bought yesterday. A loaf of bread, $3.69, the cheapest margarine, $2.79, (in Kitchener, .69¢), a few slices of cooked ham, $3.97, a dozen medium sized eggs, $2.99, etc.

9:05 PM. I met some very nice people this afternoon and evening and was able to share with them the goodness of the Lord, and to encourage them to fight the good fight of faith and be ready for the coming of the Lord.

July 4th. - 6:20 AM, 5 degrees C. I'm glad I was able to get the furnace going yesterday. By 8 AM, I'm sitting on a rock, high above Frobisher Bay, on a rocky hill east of the town. I presume it would be at least 400' above sea level. I can see for miles around. The harbour is before me where the ships come in to unload. The tide is out now and the sandy bottom stretches for at least one quarter of a mile from the shore to the water. The ship comes in on a high tide, then when the tide goes out the ship rests on the bottom. Trucks drive alongside to unload the ship. I can see the long air strip at the airport, 4 planes are visible from here, Twin Otters and 748's. It's a lovely sunny morning, but I'm glad I have my heavy winter parka on, as the wind is cold. Frobisher Bay is on a latitude of 63.45 degrees north. I am told that Nuuk in Greenland is on 64 degrees north.

At 1:05 PM I began getting ready as Wayne Moore would soon come to take me to the airport. By 2:55 PM I am on a 748 turbo prop for the flight to Greenland. At 3:40 PM we are still flying over Baffin Island. It's very rugged and mountainous with lots of snow and ice, but the weather is clear with a good view. We left the Baffin Island coast at 3:55 PM and began to cross the Davis Straits which is solid ice as far as I can see. By 4:15 PM the ice below us seemed to be broken, but all the large and small pieces appear to be frozen together. I cannot see any open water. There are a few icebergs and by 4:30 PM a cloud layer below shut out visibility to the surface.

We landed in Greenland at 5:25 PM and were taxiing to the terminal area. It's 7:25 PM here. By 10:45 PM, I'm in the Seaman Mission Hotel at the Harbour. Ships are here from Denmark and Canada and it's all open water here and for many miles West toward Baffin Island. I understand this capital city of Nuuk has about 13,000 population and all newspapers, signs and written information is in the Danish language. I've already had a good chance to witness to a Greenlander and I gave him an English New Testament as he reads English. I can see dozens of fishing boats from my window. This is a much warmer climate than Baffin Island.

July 5th. 5:30 AM in Nuuk, Greenland. It's only 3:30 AM on Baffin Island or at home in Kitchener, Ontario. The sun is high in the sky. Greenland is definitely Scandinavian - as part of Denmark. Here in Nuuk everything appears far more advanced than Baffin Island or northern Quebec. I can see dozens of boats from my window, from ordinary motorboats to sail boats, to larger inboard motor boats. The terrain is much like Baffin Island - very rocky, high hills and further inland I can see high rocky mountains with snow. At 6:05 AM the phone rang and when I answered a man said, "Good morning. Breakfast is ready!" In the harbour, I can see a Canadian ship from Halifax. It's a large fishing vessel - over here catching shrimp. It is unloading tons of shrimp into the large freezer plant just below my hotel window. At 7:00 AM I had breakfast. One Danish man said there are about 20 Kilometres of road here total. Deep fiords are all around. People use boats more than cars. One mountain near here, which I can see, is about 2500 feet high. But others nearby are over 4000 feet.

I tried at 7:20 AM to telephone another town further north, here in Greenland, where Scott Smith from Cambridge, Ontario is from; but he is now in southern Greenland with a gospel team preaching the gospel.

At 8:35 AM I boarded a Canadian fishing vessel which is unloading 415 tonnes of shrimp to be quick frozen for export. I've had good Canadian coffee and have witnessed to these men. I was also talking to a Greenland government man earlier. I witnessed to him - but he said the majority of Greenland people did not believe at all in the Bible, including himself. I asked him where he would spend eternity. He said, "I don't even think about it." At 9:30 AM, I walked up town to go to the bank to get Kroners. I talked to a Greenlander who is the first believer I've met here who knows Jesus as Saviour - others have no time to talk about spiritual things.

9:50 AM. I'm looking at an apartment building six stories high containing 68 apartments from end to end. Most of the vehicles here Japanese made, or Swedish or German and most are diesel.

11:00 AM I am on a bus touring Nuuk. The buildings have a concrete foundation here whereas on Baffin Island, they are built on pads, and have lots of air space underneath. All these streets are paved compared to pothole gravel streets in Frobisher Bay. We travel up and over the rocky hills. Some hills have the rock blasted, to cut the climb. At 11:15 AM, one driver goes off and another takes over. We are back at the town center at 11:20 AM.

By 12:05 PM, I have just eaten a Greenlander hamburger and a cup of coffee - approximately $3.00 in Canadian funds. I am in the town shopping mall where there are stores, two banks, etc. All walking area are bricks interlocked. I've talked to quite a number of people who speak English. They said the Bible and church may be alright for old folk but not for the educated young people. But I had a good opportunity to witness to them and I trust the seed sown will start to grow.

1:15 PM. On a small sight seeing boat going north. I understand the water right here is about 1300' deep. I was told the airport was built in 1979. Before that, none - only helicopter service. At 3:00 PM we came ashore where the first Danish settlement came in 1721, and Hans Edede, the priest came to do missionary work, built a house for his 27 people, lived off the land for 7 years, then found the Nuuk site and moved there in 1728.

At 4 PM we stopped at another former village built by the Danes in the 1800's. We visited the church, with the pews still here, although all the people moved to Nuuk in 1974. The Danes found homes here built by the natives with stone walls and sod roofs which they presumed were built at least 1000 years ago; but no natives were found although many graves existed. All the other tourists on this trip are Danes, so our guide is talking to them in Danish and he will explain to me in

English later. 6:30 PM and back at Nuuk. I had wonderful opportunities to witness to quite a few on the trip. One doctor was with us. He was hard to talk to because many times he said he did not believe in God, or Jesus or the Bible. But it was a challenge to me and he listened to what I had to say. He said: "I still do not believe, no matter what you say." But I pray that the Holy Spirit will cause the seed sown to grow and bring forth fruit. Some others were more receptive and again, I know the seed was sown, and as I've been faithful to do the best I can, I know God is faithful to do His part. Those on ship - including the Captain and our guide heard the gospel story, perhaps some for the first time. I advised them to get a Bible and read it faithfully every day. The sun just went below the top of a hill north of here at 10:55 PM, (it does not set in the west) but it's still shining on the high hills east of here. It will be day light all night and the sun will appear above the hills about 3:00 AM. I awakened at 2:45 AM to see the sun just peaking over the top of the hills due east from here.

July 6th. Got up at 7:00 AM. By 9:50 I've been out meeting people, trying to find someone who speaks and reads English. One young fellow spoke fairly good English. I began to witness to him about Jesus. He said, "I've got no time for these things." So, away he went. I went to a gas and diesel station - one litre of diesel is approximately .35¢ Canadian. One fine young man who attends University in Denmark, has been working for the summer holidays and speaks and reads English. He was nice to talk to and listened to me share the gospel. He accepted an English New Testament from me and promised to read it. At 12:30 PM in downtown Nuuk, I've talked to quite a few people but they have no time to talk about the Lord. I've just come out of a gift shop where I was looking for a gift to take to my wife. One of the sales persons was a fine young lady from Denmark. She speaks and reads English. I witnessed to her. She said, "My girl friend and I have just been talking about these things." She was glad to receive my last English New Testament and she promised to read it for sure.

At 3:25 PM I was standing beside the oldest house in Nuuk of modern time. Built in 1728 of stone by the first missionary who came to Greenland, Hans Edede. The woodwork has been changed and repaired but the stone walls are original. One man is here to do some repair. I tried to witness to him but he said, "I don't believe that. Who knows?" The premier of Greenland now lives in this house.

July 7th. - 4:45 AM Sunday. The weather is OO - heavy fog - down to the ground. In my opinion, this fog typifies the heavy spiritual darkness that covers the people of Greenland.

Yesterday I met people from other towns and villages who were visiting Nuuk, the capital. I tried to talk with them, but found they considered themselves far superior in knowledge than to believe there is a God and a Saviour. But before we parted I let them know there is a Heaven to gain and a hell to shun. I believe seed was sown and I pray it will germinate and grow.

The fog began to dissipate at 8:35 AM and I could see men working on the docks below, unloading fish.

10:10 AM. Two of the Sea Man's Mission hotel staff brought me to the Lutheran church. The service is in Greenlandic language, similar to the Inuit language of Canada, but somewhat different. Most of the people here are native but quite a few white people of Danish Descent.

By 10:50 AM many more people were coming in, some dressed in their beautiful Greenlandic costumes. Beaded capes across their shoulders and down to the waist, fur trousers and beaded leggings. There are two or three babies to be baptized. At 11:20 AM two Greenlanders were before the minister. I presume it was a wedding ceremony. The woman was dressed in the Greenlandic costume of the colourful beaded cape, fur trousers and beaded skin leggings. I was back at the hotel by 12:15 PM and the Lutheran minister rode with us about half way. I asked him what it would cost to buy one of these beaded capes. He told me over $1000.00 Canadian.

At 3:15 PM I was at the dock watching the Greenlanders unload hundreds of pounds of shrimp and also small cod, about two feet long. I found two people who could speak English and they appeared interested in the gospel. I promised to send them literature in English. Then I went into the government cooler to see two men take the heavy crates of shrimp and dump them into a screened vat. They stir the shrimp to wash them, then dump them into crates. They are weighed and the man who owns the fishing boat gets paid per pound or kilo by the government. By 3:55 PM I've been in the plant with so many complicated machines, which cut the heads and tails off and fillet the fish, which pass on a massive conveyor belt, with many Greenland men and women trimming the fillets that go into trays, are weighed and go into the freezer ready for market. At 4:30 PM the temperature was 15 1/2 degrees C., a beautiful day.

At 7:45 PM I was in a Brethren Church. I went to a Pentecostal Church, but they had cancelled their services for the summer, so we were here for the evening service. They sang in Danish and one of the songs was "He Lives, He Lives".

I was back at the hotel by 9:50 PM. The pastor at the

church preached in Danish for about 20 minutes. Another hymn was sung. Then the song leader preached for about 15 minutes. The pastor closed in prayer. I met someone who could speak English, and one family invited me over tomorrow.

July 8th. - 6:50 AM. A very large ship came in last night and it is at the dock. By 8:45 AM I found out it was a huge ship from Finland, an oil tanker. It had just finished unloading oil and gas from Denmark and was to leave in a few minutes. for Montreal, then to Sarnia to load up again. The name on the side was Tavi - Naantalie, Nesteship. It's one of the newest and largest tankers, built in Turku, Finland. I was on board and met some of the crew members.

11:05 AM. I've been on board a very large shrimp factory ship. A Greenlander showed me how they get the shrimp in nets, haul them on board, wash them, grade them, cook some for export and then freeze them. They freeze some to 30 degrees below zero for export to Japan. I tried to witness to my guide about the love of God, but his limited knowledge of English confined us to basics.

7:15 PM. I had good opportunities to share the good news to quite a few people. Some resisted the idea of God and the Bible completely. Others said, they did not know, but they appeared interested and I explained God's love in Jesus and the plan of salvation. I promised to send some literature to a few of those who appeared interested. Now I must pack up for my flight tomorrow morning.

July 9th. 3:50 AM and the sun is coming up and fishing boats are on the go. I believe men work here night and day, loading and unloading. I had better get all my things packed and ready to go. 6:40 AM. Just had my breakfast and now waiting for my friend to come and pick me up and take me to the airport - he works there. I met a lady from Timmins, Ontario. She has been painting here in Greenland and is flying back this morning. I board the 748 turbo jet at 7:55 AM to fly back to Canada. The lady from Timmins and two others who are professional painters and travel the Arctic to paint are also on board. Soon we are flying over thousands of rocky islands. At 8:10 AM we are flying over fog and by 8:25 AM it's open water. By 9:00 AM we are about half way to Baffin Island, flying over a lot of floating ice which becomes thicker as we approach Canada flying south west. To our right is a large mass of ice as far as I can see.

9:40 AM. It would take a large ice breaker to break through the ice below and open a path for a ship. This is so much different than on the west coast of Greenland, which is ice free the year round. It's solid ice below. I was able to talk to a Greenlander at the airport before leaving Nuuk. He said he does not believe the Bible nor in God, "that's the white man's new idea - our old customs and ways are better. I will never change." They seem to be a very proud race of people. And I thank God for the opportunity of witnessing to a good number of them and will send gospel literature to some who appeared somewhat interested. At 10:15 which is 8:15 here in Frobisher Bay, we've just landed and will turn around and taxi into the terminal.

By 1:00 PM, I'm on a 737 jet flying to Fort Chimo. At 1:40 it's solid ice below in Ungava Bay. We land at Fort Chimo at 2:00 PM and it's a beautiful day here too.

I'm in an Inuit home at 5:50 PM and we are having a Bible study. At 6:30 PM I am finding we have to go slowly. One Inuit understands more English than another so they try to explain it to one another. I've never stopped in their home before but now I know why I am here. One of them just mentioned how much they thanked God for sending me here and 15 minutes later, 2 Inuit women accept Jesus as their Saviour with tears flowing. We went on to studying more until 9:20 PM when we concluded our Bible Study in prayer.

July 10th. - 6:50 AM and time to get up and make some breakfast. Last evening I bought a few groceries at the Co-op store. It was a good breakfast. I boiled some eggs, made toast and coffee, then I washed the dishes as the other folk were still sleeping.

10:45 AM and we are having another Bible Study. The theme being, "how to live to please God." At 12 noon it was time to close in prayer as some have to return home to prepare lunch and I have to get my things ready to go to the airport.

At 2:15 PM I'm on a 727 jet for Montreal. I met Inuits at the airport in Ft. Chimo from many villages in Northern Quebec. By 6:50 PM we're waiting for my luggage in the Toronto airport. Tyyne and Dan have come for me and I'll be glad to be back home.

Mission accomplished! Thanks to your prayers and financial support which has made this missionary trip possible. God bless you!

The main reason for missionary work is to win souls to Jesus. That is why Jesus died on the cross of Calvary - to pay the penalty for all of our sins.

John 3:16 *"For God so loved the world, that He gave His only begotten Son, that whosoever believeth in Him should not perish, but have everlasting life."*

You see the choice is ours - either to believe and accept Jesus, or to reject Him.

2 Peter 3:9 *"The Lord is not slack concerning His promise, as some men count slackness; but is longsuffering to usward,*

not willing that any should perish, but that all should come to repentance."

1 John 1:9 *"If we confess our sins, He is faithful and just to forgive us our sins, and to cleanse us from all unrighteousness."*

We thank God for the millions around the world who have accepted Jesus as Saviour, and are now ready to meet the Lord, either by death or the rapture.

1 Thessalonians 4:16 - 17 *"For the Lord Himself shall descend from heaven with a shout, with the voice of the archangel, and with the trump of God: and the dead in Christ shall rise first: Then we which are alive and remain shall be caught up together with them in the clouds to meet the Lord in the air: and so shall we ever be with the Lord."*

I must add a warning to all - that Satan, our enemy is consistently trying to deceive the Christians.

1 Timothy 4:1 *"Now the Spirit speaketh expressly, that in the latter times some shall depart from the faith, giving heed to seducing spirits, and doctrines of devils."*

So we see that some shall depart from the faith and will miss the rapture, and will be left behind to go through the great tribulation when the antichrist shall rule the world.

Revelation 13:16 - 17 *"And he causeth all, both small and great, rich and poor, free and bond, to receive a mark in their right hand, or in their foreheads: And that no man might buy or sell, save he that had the mark, or the name of the beast, or the number of his name."*

What happens if one takes the mark?

Revelation 14:9 - 10 *"If any man worship the beast, and his image, and receive his mark in his forehead, or in his hand, The same shall drink the wrath of God, which is poured out without mixture into the cup of His indignation; and he shall be tormented with fire and brimstone in the presence of the holy angels, and in the presence of the Lamb."*

So we see here that if one misses the rapture and be left behind, each one will be compelled to take the mark of the beast. And if one refuses, than what?

Revelation 20:4 *"I saw the souls of them that were beheaded for the witness of Jesus, and for the word of God, and which had not worshipped the beast, neither his image, neither had received this mark upon their foreheads, or in their hands; and they lived and reigned with Christ a thousand years."*

We find here, that in order to buy or sell, one must have the mark of the beast. But if one takes the mark, he is doomed forever. So it's better to refuse the mark and by so doing, this scripture tells us that one will be beheaded. It is far better to have one's head cut off, then that one will be resurrected to join others who are with Christ, to rule and reign with Him for a thousand years, after which we shall have a new heaven and new earth.

Matthew 24:44 *"Therefore be ye also ready: for in such an hour as ye think not the Son of man cometh."*

A Parting Word

Isaiah 55:9. "For as the Heavens are higher than the earth - so are my ways higher than yours and my thoughts than your thoughts."

January 24th., 1992. Cape Coral, Florida. I had planned to be away, up in the Arctic at this time, but instead, I am here in Florida. I had purchased tickets for myself and Udjualuk, my Eskimo interpreter, and James, a fellow Gospel preacher had bought his own ticket as he wanted to go with me. We were to leave here on January 7th and return on February 13th.

On December 28th I was rushed to the Cape Coral hospital with chest pains. After many tests, I was transferred to Fort Myers hospital on January 5th, and the next day I had open heart surgery - a triple by pass. I was sent home on January 12th, way ahead of schedule because they said I had recovered so rapidly.

But, in the meantime, I had phoned Udjualuk and James to go ahead without me and carry out our plans. They flew to the last Eskimo village nearest the North Pole and began to work south to as many Eskimo villages as possible before returning home on February 13th. I've received word that they are doing this and God is blessing in the services.

I thank the Lord that I didn't have this health experience in the Arctic. I am getting stronger each day but it will take some time to get back to normal.

As the Scripture says, *Gods ways are higher than our ways,* so we accept that and go accordingly.

Philippians 3:13 &14. "Brethren, I count not myself to have apprehended: but this one thing I do, forgetting those things which are behind, and reaching forth unto those things which are before, I press toward the mark of the high calling of God in Christ Jesus.

Rev. John Spillenaar
703-24 Midland Dr.
Kitchener, ON   N2A 2A8